Hearts West

True Stories of Mail-Order Brides on the Frontier

CHRIS ENSS

TWODOT®

GUILFORD, CONNECTICUT
HELENA, MONTANA
AN IMPRINT OF THE GLOBE PEQUOT PRESS

A · T W O D O T® · B O O K

Copyright © 2005 by Chris Enss

Text design: Lisa Reneson

Library of Congress Cataloging-in-Publication Data
Enss, Chris, 1961–
     Hearts West: true stories of mail-order brides on the frontier/Chris Enss.
—1st ed.
         p. cm.
     "A TwoDot book"—T.p. verso.
     Includes bibliographical references.
     ISBN 0-7627-2756-X
     1. Marriage brokerage—West (U.S.)—History. 2. Mail order brides—West (U.S.)—Bibliography. 3. Women pioneers—West (U.S.)—Biography. 4. Frontier and pioneer life—West (U.S.) 5. West (U.S.)—Social life and customs. 6. West (U.S.)—Bibliography. I. Title.

HQ802.E575 2005
306.82—dc22   2005046363

Manufactured in the United States of America
First Edition/First Printing

CONTENTS

For My Grandma Edna
Who Possesses the Kindest Heart in the East and the West

ACKNOWLEDGMENTS

When I was a teenager, the notion of advertising for a spouse inspired me to use the technique to find a date for the Junior–Senior Prom. The ad I placed in the school newspaper read like this:

> **Wanted:** A date to the Junior–Senior Prom. If even slightly interested in attending this year's big event, please meet me in front of the school library at lunch time.

Fourteen girls in the same situation as I was showed up, hoping there would be an onslaught of boys who wanted to go to the dance. Alas, only one boy stopped by the library and he was waiting for members of the chess club to meet him and get a game going.

And so I begin my thanks and recognition to the Buena High School newspaper editor who allowed me to so boldly tell my classmates I was dateless and needed help. In writing this book, fond memories of that experience washed over me and helped me to identify, on a small level, with the mail-order brides of the West.

I received a great deal of assistance from the librarians at the California State Library in Sacramento and the Madelyn Helling Library in Nevada City. Researchers at historical libraries from Arizona to New York happily shared many of the documents used to create this book. In particular I would like to express my gratitude to Shane Molander at the State Historical Society of North Dakota; Delores Henry at the Public Library in New Bedford, Massachusetts; and Julia Davis Park at the Idaho Black History Museum. Without their generous contributions this material would not be complete. Thank you also to JoAnn Chartier for adding to the content of the book and seeing me through the process.

And finally, thank you to my editors Stephanie Hester and Megan Hiller for their perseverance and direction. I appreciate all you have done.

FOREWORD

*T*he impact of women on the American frontier in the nineteenth and early twentieth centuries should not be underestimated. To a large degree, women were responsible for taming the wilderness of the "Wild West." Under their influence, churches were formed, schools and libraries were established, and the importance of home and hearth was rediscovered. The result was nothing short of a complete transformation, the conversion of the western frontier from a rowdy, male-dominated society into a place that became a mecca for settlement even after the Gold Rush and the promise of cheap land came to an end. During these early years of western development, women often worked right alongside their men, turning the soil, planting the crops, and caring for the children who came along.

It didn't take long for men who had traveled to far-off places west of the Mississippi to recognize that their desire and need of the "gentler sex" was profound. It is this desire and need that leads us now to the wonderful compilation before us.

Hearts West reveals the real-life tales of women who became mail-order brides. Also presented are the stories of those enterprising few who attempted to make their fortune by bringing young women, spinsters, and widows to would-be husbands in the West. By the 1850s, so enticing was the call to riches that there were more eligible bachelors in the West than there were in the East. Some women, after answering a mail-order request, were taken out to the new land by their intended. Others traveled alone overland or by sea. Many of the latter became seasick and would remain so for the length of the voyage. As we shall see in the unfolding set of stories brought together here for our enjoyment and education, not all of the matches were successful. All of them, however, contributed to the rich and colorful history of the West's early years.

—Mary Ann Trygg
Madelyn Helling Branch Librarian, Nevada City, Calif.
(and proud granddaughter of a Dakota Territory pioneering family)

INTRODUCTION

*Unmarried miners in these parts showed a consciousness of being
somewhat the worse for a long, rough journey West in which they
had lived semi-barbarous lives, and for their continued
separation from the amenities and refinements of home.*

Sarah Royce
Placerville, California—1852

The promise of boundless acres of land in the West lured hundreds of
men away from farms, businesses, and homes in the eastern states as tales of
early explorers and fur trappers filtered back from the frontier. Thousands
more headed for California after hearing the siren call of Gold! Tracts of
timber in the Northwest and a farming paradise in the Willamette Valley of
Oregon had even more people packing up and leaving home for the promised land.

The vast acres and the trees and the gold were all there, and men set
about carving their place in the wilderness. By the early 1850s, western
adventurers lifted their heads and looked around and realized one vital element was missing from the bountiful western territories: women.

"A woman's track was discovered in the road leading to Mormon
Island. The track of a woman was such a novel thing the boys enclosed it
with sticks (you know women were scarce in California in those days), sang,

Bowman & Lee,

NO. 906 MAIN STREET,

{Duplicates of this Photo
{can be had at any time.

PENDLETON, OREGON.

Unidentified sisters dressed in their Sunday finery submitted this photograph to the San Francisco edition of The Matrimonial News *in 1882.*

danced, telling yarns and giving cheers to the woman's track in the dust until a late hour in the evening," recalled Henry Bigler, third governor of California.

Eliza Farnham, recognizing that she was no beauty, nevertheless was astonished to be the target of admiring eyes wherever she went in the Gold Country in 1849. Shocked at the dissolute lives of the largely male inhabitants of California, she conceived a plan to bring proper ladies to the West, which she saw as badly in need of the civilizing hand of woman. Her plan included a rigorous application process to guarantee only the most virtuous ladies would arrive on the good ship *Angelique*. The plan was widely publicized and endorsed by clergymen and officials. With anticipation running high, hundreds of angry bachelors nearly started a riot when just three ladies tiptoed down the gangplank in San Francisco.

In Washington Territory, where men outnumbered women nine to one in the 1850s and 1860s, a scheme to ship respectable women and families to the shores of Puget Sound was hatched by Asa Mercer. He raised money for the first trip, traveled to the eastern seaboard, and in 1864 brought his first shipload of marriageable women to Seattle. Only eleven women disembarked, leaving a lot of disillusioned bachelors. Mercer's second trip in 1866 netted a larger cargo of potential brides, but that trip was to be his last attempt at supplying a rather urgent demand.

Newspapers editorialized about the lack of marriageable females: "We want an emigration of respectable females to California: of rosy-cheeked 'down east' Yankee girls—of stout 'hoosier' and 'badger' lasses, who shall be wives to our farmers and mechanics, and mothers to a generation of 'Yankee Californians,'" opined the editor of the *Alta California* newspaper in 1851.

The *Matrimonial News*, a San Francisco matchmaking newspaper, was dedicated to "promoting honorable matrimonial engagements and true conjugal facilities" for men and women through personal advertisements, and was a forerunner of the matchmaking clubs and personal ads in newspapers today. Not all of the matrimonial bureaus and agencies were legitimate, however, and many a disappointed bride or groom was left with empty pockets after contracting for a mail-order mate.

Mail-order bride Elinore Pruitt, a widow from Arkansas, married Clyde Stewart after answering his ad in the *News*. The two were happily married for more than twenty years. Eleanor Berry was not as lucky. Her mail-order husband misrepresented himself in his letters and the marriage lasted less than an hour.

In Arizona, shootouts over the few eligible females led to the establishment of clubs devoted to arranging marriages. Six Tucson wives met in 1885 and formed the Busy Bee Club. Convinced that marriage would spread calm among the black miners starved for the comforts of home, they met to recruit suitable women to marry the town's unruly bachelors. Some of the men were old enough to be the fathers or grandfathers of the teenagers they selected as their brides. Once the vows were exchanged, these young women often took on a houseful of children as well as a husband.

Hearts West contains the stories of men and women longing for the tie that binds, who risked everything in making an alliance with a virtual stranger. Some married well; some lost everything. Some, like Seattle's Mercer Maids, became integral parts of the history of a specific region. Others may be anonymous, yet all deserve to be remembered for helping to civilize the rugged frontier.

MARY RICHARDSON & ELKANAH WALKER

The Missionaries

*Is it advisable for me to go out [West] without a
companion? This is rather a delicate question to ask. But as
I view it of such importance, it will plead its own apology.*

Missionary Elkanah Walker's letter to the
American Missions Board
—March 16, 1837

*You ought by all means, to have a good, healthy, patient,
well-informed devotedly pious wife. There is a Mary
Richardson of Baldwin, Maine, who has offered herself to
the [Missionary] Board, but we cannot send her single.
From her testimony, I should think her a good girl. If you
have nobody in view, you might inquire about her.*

American Missions Board Secretary William Armstrong's
response to Elkanah Walker—March 20, 1837

A bright, blinding sunrise lit the small Richardson farm one April morning in Baldwin, Maine, in 1837. Mary Richardson, the eldest daughter of the family, stood in the living room folding her father's discarded newspapers. Casting a glance out the front window, she squinted hard into the haze that was turning the valley into a trembling distortion of itself. A cloud mercifully drifted in front of the sun and Mary was able to make out two riders approaching the house. She recognized one man to be a family friend, Dr. Lewis Whitney. The other rider was a stranger.

Assuming the men were on their way to visit her father, the twenty-six-year-old woman continued on with her housework. Moments later, her sister summoned her to the parlor to receive Dr. Whitney's companion, a lean, lanky gentlemen who had come to call on her. Once pleasantries were exchanged, a letter of introduction was presented to Mary.

As good fortune would have it I have learned today of an opportunity to send a line near you at least, by the bearer Mr. Walker and perhaps he will pass through Baldwin in which case I have invited him to call at your Father's on my account . . . If you receive this line, you will receive it as an introduction of the bearer - Mr. E. Walker to your kind regards, as a suitor for your heart and hand.

Should he thus present himself to you, the act will not be so hasty on his part as might at first seem - he has not been wholly unacquainted with you - though personally unknown.

Friend and fellow missionary student William Thayer
—April 17, 1837

Mary looked up from Thayer's letter and smiled a guarded smile at the bashful man. He shifted uncomfortably in his seat as Mary continued reading.

Elkanah Walker is a fine man and has been appointed by the American Board to go as a missionary to the Zoolah [sic] mission in South East [sic], Africa . . . Of his disposition . . . without flattery or puffing I number it among the kindest . . . Of his talents I cannot predicate any thing more than respectability. He is not brilliant, but he is exceedingly tormented with diffidence and therefore his first appearance speaks less for him than after-acquaintance would justify. In short, he is one of those men who must be known in order to be justly appreciated. As for his manners - look for yourself. If you can put up with somewhat of the uncultivated—If you can get by that obtrusive awkwardness which he

Mary was moved by the sentiment in the letter, but knew she would need to know more about this suitor before she could fully pass judgment. Based on looks alone Mary was unimpressed. She described him in her journal as being "a tall and rather awkward gentleman."

Elkanah stood at six-foot-four and was quite self-conscious of his height. He was painfully shy and unassuming, so much so his friends said it was hard for him to even say amen at the end of his prayers. He was born on August 7, 1805, in North Yarmouth, Maine. He grew up on a farm, attended church regularly, and was the sixth child in a family of ten. From an early age he aspired to be a pastor. He entered the ministry shortly after he turned seventeen.

Elkanah and Mary shared a zeal for serving the Lord. Born on April 1, 1811, Mary knew by the age of ten that she would become a missionary. Like Elkanah, she also came from a large family; she had eleven brothers and sisters. After excelling in all her subjects at school and graduating with high marks, she went on to attend seminary. Once her formal training in missions was complete, she applied to the American Missions Board for a position in the West, but because she was single, her request was denied. Mary was deeply distressed over her circumstances. She briefly contemplated a proposal of marriage from a neighboring farmer, but he was not interested in the missions.

Doctor Whitney and Elkanah Walker's visit that spring morning was brief. The men made their goodbyes and left Mary alone to reflect on the meeting. That evening she recorded her thoughts in her journal.

His remarks were good. But not delivered in a style the most energetic. After meeting, instead of shaking hands in a free cordial kind of way as I was anticipating, his attention seemed rather taken up in some other way . . . I saw nothing particularly interesting or disagreeable in the man, tho I pretty much made up my mind that he was not a missionary, but rather an ordinary kind of unaspiring man who was anxious to be looking up a settlement.

Mary Richardson—April 22, 1837

In spite of the uncomfortable first meeting, Elkanah dared to return to the Richardson home later that same evening with Reverend Noah Emerson, pastor of the local Congregational Church. The men were to attend a missions meeting in the area and stay over at the Richardsons' home. The following morning Mary and Elkanah had occasion to sit and talk about their desire to be missionaries to the "heathens." After discussing their lives and discovering they shared a mutual friend, Elkanah made his intentions known to Mary.

"I suppose I am an accepted missionary," he told her. "As I have no one engaged to go with me on my journey, I have come with the intention of offering myself to you." Mary blushed, taken aback by his candor. Before she could respond to his bold declaration, her mother entered the room where the two were seated and invited them to join the other family members for breakfast prayer. Once the prayers were concluded, Mary excused herself from the others and returned to her room to think about the morning's events.

The opportunity to serve the Lord as a missionary was appealing, but she questioned the wisdom of becoming engaged to a mere stranger.

Mary Richardson

The conflict was rather severe. The hand of Providence appeared so plain that I could not but feel that there was something like duty about it, and yet how to go to work to feel satisfied and love him, I hardly know. But concluded the path of duty must prove the path of peace. I could discover a good foundation for true friendship.

Mary Richardson—April 23, 1837

After much prayer and deliberation, Mary accepted Elkanah's proposal. During their short engagement, the two spent countless hours taking long walks and buggy rides and talking. They shared their dreams and stories of their pasts with one another and within a month's time, they had fallen in love.

His affection for me appears to be becoming very strong and somewhat enthusiastic, and I think I love him full well enough. We sat up for the first time after eleven, that is to say until one, at the close of our interview he exclaimed: "This is the happiest evening I have ever passed. I can be happy anywhere if my Mary is with me.

I feel the angels are contemplating our conduct with pleasure."

Mary Richardson—May 27, 1837

In June 1837, Elkanah said goodbye to his intended and traveled to Bangor, Maine, to complete his seminary training. During their five-month absence from one another, they sent letters back and forth, outlining plans for their life after their wedding and expressing their affections.

I love you, therefore I want you. If I could be with you this moment a more heartfelt kiss you never had than I would bestow. To fold you in my arms, hear from your faithful lips that I am still your dearest one would be sweet, sweet indeed.

Elkanah Walker—August 18, 1837

On Tuesday, November 7, Elkanah appeared unexpectedly at the Richardsons' home. Mary was thrilled to see her fiancé, and after supper the two enjoyed a beautiful moonlit walk. His visit was short, but he promised they would be together soon and onto serving the Lord. Shortly before Christmas, Mary received a letter from Elkanah with news of their joint missionary assignment. She recorded her sentiments in her journal. "The Board wishes him to go beyond the Rocky Mountains. The proposal strikes me favorable . . . They wish to be ready to start in April. I hope we shall be able to go."

Between letters Elkanah had traveled to Independence, Missouri, to purchase supplies and make preparations for their journey across the plains. From there, he wrote to inform his soon-to-be bride what she needed to pack for the trip.

A change of clothes is all we want. Buckskin drawers are the best for riding on horseback. Our ladies should also have drawers to prevent being chafed in riding. We should carry no baggage excepting such as what we want to wear or use on the journey . . . all the baggage we carry will cost us one dollar per pound.

Elkanah Walker—December 18, 1837

The missionary board told Mary and Elkanah to be ready to leave for the West by March 20, 1838. The pair then decided to wed earlier than originally planned. They exchanged vows on Monday, March 5, at 11:00 A.M. in front of a small audience of friends and family. It was a Richardson tradition that brides wore black during their wedding ceremonies to symbolize the grief over parting from their relatives. When Mary bid farewell to her parents that day, it was the last time she ever saw them alive.

The newlyweds left Independence heading to Oregon on April 23, 1838. They were deeply devoted to one another and excited about the adventures that lay ahead of them. Four months later they reached the Tshimakain Mission in Waiilatpu, Oregon. While en route to their new home, Mary gave birth to the first of their seven children.

The Walkers served as ministers to the Pacific Northwest Indians for more than nine years. They left the area after natives attacked the mission and killed many of the missionaries living there. The couple relocated to Forest Grove, where Elkanah took a position as pastor for the local church. He later helped found the Tualatin Academy, which later became Pacific University.

When Elkanah died in 1877, Mary missed her husband terribly and recorded thoughts about her loss in the journal she had started five years prior to their marriage.

It seems as though I can't live without my husband. I feel so lonely. I think of so many things I want to tell Mr. Walker. I realize more and more how much more I loved him than anyone else.

Mary Walker—December 18, 1877

Mary passed away twenty years after her beloved Elkanah. The relationship, which had begun in writing, endured for close to four decades.

ELEANOR BERRY & LOUIS DREIBELBIS
The Schoolmarm and the Scoundrel

Lonesome miner wants wife to share stake and prospects. Please respond to Louis Dreibelbis in Grass Valley, California.

San Francisco Magazine
—April 12, 1873

*P*lease come out, Eleanor," the frail voice of an elderly Ida Eigleberry pleaded from one side of a closed door. She knocked lightly, but urgently, on the frame. There was no answer. Ida turned the knob and gently pushed the door open. Her senses were immediately assaulted with chloroform fumes.

Choking back violent coughs, she made her way to a still body on the other side of the suite. Twenty-two-year-old Eleanor Berry was face down on the mattress, with a handkerchief covering her head. The old woman quickly evaluated the desperate scene and panicked, racing out into the hallway. "Norman!" Ida called out to her husband. "Run and get the doctor. I'm afraid our Eleanor has gone and done something foolish."

According to the historical publication *The Californians,* if Eleanor Berry had gotten her wish, she would have expired a month earlier, on July 27, 1873. She reasoned that if her life had ended on her wedding day, she might have escaped the degradation and heartbreak that was to come. But alas, God had not struck her dead and now the deed was left to her.

Eleanor's life began in the spring of 1851 in Gilroy, California. Her parents died when she was an infant and so she was raised by her neighbors, the Eigleberrys. She grew to be an attractive young lady, and chose to teach school as her profession. Still single at the age of twenty-two and fearing she always would be, Eleanor responded to an advertisement posted in a Bay Area literary journal. Louis Dreibelbis, the author of the advertisement, was searching for a wife and was thrilled to receive Eleanor's letter in response to his ad. In the advertisement, Louis described himself as a wealthy, average-looking man eager to settle down.

Letters between the two went back and forth from Eleanor's home in Gilroy to Louis's in Grass Valley. The pair corresponded for three months. She was quite taken with his candor and his praise of her desire to work with children. "Such a woman will make a fine mother," he wrote. Louis found Eleanor's letters to be "intelligent and sincere in tone."

It did not take long for the mutual attraction to evolve into affection. Louis's letter of proposal was met with enthusiastic acceptance, and the couple decided on a wedding date of July 27, 1873. After resigning her position as Gilroy's schoolmistress, Eleanor packed her trunk and boarded an east-bound train to meet Louis for the first time and marry him.

Eleanor fanned herself with a newspaper as she took her seat on the train. The temperature inside the Central Pacific passenger car was oppressive, hotter even than the ninety-five degrees outside the train. She was accompanied by several passengers making their way to the mining camps near Grass Valley in Nevada County. Once the train reached Colfax, the bride-to-be and her belongings were transferred to a six-horse stagecoach. Of the thirteen passengers on board, Eleanor was the only woman.

The stage driver promised Eleanor and the other passengers a safe trip and tried to assure them that they would not be overtaken by highwaymen, men who robbed travelers on public roads. Given the cargo, the driver no doubt needed to reassure himself of that notion as well. Nestled between the trunks and suitcases was a safe containing $7,000 in gold that was to be deposited into a Grass Valley bank.

The trip was relatively uneventful for the first leg of the journey. According to one newspaper account, the passengers passed the time on the eight-hour journey swapping stories about the places they had lived or visited. Eleanor contributed to the conversation as well, trading brilliant remarks and witty banter with other passengers. The men admired her "vivacity and charm."

During lulls in the conversation, Eleanor daydreamed about her upcoming nuptials and life thereafter. She removed a few of Louis's letters from her handbag and reread them. She smiled to herself, imagining she and her betrothed standing at the altar, looking into one another's eyes, and seeing all the possibilities to come. The coach's abrupt stop brought her back to the present, tossing her on the floor in the stagecoach.

A gruff voice outside the buggy demanded the passengers step out with their hands in the air. She exchanged anxious glances with her wide-eyed travel companions, as they reluctantly did as they were told.

Four armed men wearing gunnysack masks over their heads shouted at the passengers. The bandits eyed their victims carefully. For a moment no one made a move. Then the driver lowered his arms a bit and a highwayman with a six-shooter pulled the hammer back on his gun. The driver's arms shot back up.

"We'll take your treasure box," the man with the six-shooter demanded.

"It's on the other stage," the driver insisted.

The bandit snickered. "Then we'll keep you here until the other stage comes around," he warned.

The driver studied the dress of the bandits for a quick moment. Their feet were encased in gunnysacks and tied in place at the ankle, a trick professionals used so no visible footprints would be left for a posse to follow. The driver realized these were ruthless desperados who would make good on their threats, and he finally relented. "It's no use fooling any longer," he said. "This is the only stage tonight."

The man with the six-shooter snickered again. "That's what we thought."

A bandit carrying a shotgun aimed the barrel of the weapon at the driver's head and motioned for him to move away from the stage. The two other thieves instructed the passengers to do the same.

After lining the travelers up against a nearby fence, the gunmen climbed on top of the stage and headed for the strongbox attached to the coach. Several attempts were made to break into the safe with a pick, but to no avail. The thieves decided to blow the lock with gunpowder.

Eleanor looked on in horror as one of the men hauled a small canister of gunpowder from his saddlebag on the stage. The safe was in direct proximity to the passengers' luggage. An explosion would destroy the trunks and all of their belongings.

"Stop," Eleanor yelled. The men halted their work to listen to the prospective bride. "Gentlemen, my trousseau is in my trunk. Won't you take it down before you blow up the coach?"

The thief with the six-shooter stood up and backed away from the safe. "With pleasure, miss," he replied. Eleanor walked over to the stage as the robber chief jumped off and motioned for the gunman near the safe to toss her trunk down. As he reached up to take hold of the trunk, Eleanor noticed a long, jagged scar on the back of the man's hand. She filed the image away in her mind and was pleased at the sight of her possessions being returned to her. The highwayman turned away and went about his business.

KABOOOOOOMMMM!!!

Seconds after the robbers lit the fuse on the canister of gunpowder, a fierce explosion ripped through the stagecoach. The thieves wasted no time searching through the rubble to find the gold. After securing their ill-gotten gain in their saddlebags, the leader hopped on the back of his horse. "Come on!" he yelled to his cohorts. Following suit, the gunmen leapt onto their rides and all four hurried off into the trees, disappearing from sight.

The shaken driver inspected the damage to his coach and determined that the frame of the stage and the running gear were still intact. The spooked horses were settled and readied to continue the journey to Grass Valley. The passengers found their places on the shattered coach and they were off.

Upon their arrival in Nevada City, the crime was quickly reported to authorities, and police officers immediately set out to apprehend the culprits. The stage then proceeded on to its appointed destinations, first depositing Eleanor at the cottage of her betrothed.

Louis Dreibelbis's landlady greeted the exhausted bride and informed her that her fiancé had been called out of town but would return shortly. The kind woman escorted Eleanor into a room where she could prepare for the wedding.

The bride-to-be washed away the dust and dirt from her travels with a bath the landlady drew for her. Afterward, she dressed in her most elegant attire, pinned up her hair, and made up her face.

"It's time, dear," the landlady said as she burst into the bedroom. Eleanor quickly stood up, smoothed down her dress, and checked her look in the mirror. The next time she saw her reflection she would be Mrs. Louis Dreibelbis.

Eleanor entered the parlor smiling nervously. There were two men sitting off to one side, a minister and a witness. Opposite the pair, Louis stood dressed in his Sunday best. The pair sized each other up for the first time. He looked considerably older than she expected, but there was a strength of character in his face that she always imagined her husband would have. Louis, on the other hand, was taken aback for a moment, almost as if he was surprised to see her. He covered his response with a slight smile before drinking in the petite, agreeable features of his fiancé.

The minister took his place in front of a fireplace and the bride and groom made their way toward him. The minister happily opened the Bible he was holding and began the proceedings. As the couple recited their vows to one another, Eleanor paused between pledges to think. Louis's voice sounded strangely familiar.

"We've been corresponding for months," she told herself. "Perhaps what I recognize is the echo of the idea of him in my head." The minister pronounced the two "man and wife" and Louis timidly leaned in to kiss his spouse. Their embrace was brief and awkward. The minister rescued them from the tense moment by escorting the newlyweds to a table to sign the marriage license.

Eleanor took the ink pen in hand and placed her name in the appropriate area. Louis followed suit once she passed him the pen. As he signed his name, the light from the flames in the fireplace reflected off his hand revealing a long, jagged scar. Eleanor knew in an instant where she'd seen the mark before. The color drained from her face and she screamed. She hurried out of the parlor and locked herself in her assigned quarters.

Louis looked on, stunned, not knowing what to say or do. Of course he had recognized Eleanor as the young woman on the stage he robbed earlier, but he could not imagine that she had recognized him. He raced out of the home, mounted his horse, and rode off into the night, saying nothing to the landlady, minister, or witness when he left.

The landlady pressed her ear to the bedroom door and listened for a sound on the other side. Eleanor was crying. Too ashamed to face anyone and wishing she would simply expire, she remained holed up in the room until the next morning.

The unfortunate bride stepped into the parlor the next day, her face wet with tears. The minister and landlady greeted her with apologies and words of comfort. Eleanor looked at them confused. "Mr. Dreibelbis and I never married," she told her compassionate new friends. "I have no memory of a wedding, only a dream that in the night I was carried off by robbers."

The minister and the landlady exchanged worried glances, assuming that the shock from the previous day's events had left her disoriented. "I've changed my mind about taking Mr. Dreibelbis as my husband," she told the pair before her. "He's not as well-fixed as I expected to find him."

After packing her trunk and soliciting a ride to the stage stop from the minister, Eleanor was on her way back to her home in Gilroy.

Nevada County Sheriff's deputies caught up with Louis Dreibelbis more than two months after the wedding. He confessed to his crime, turned state's evidence, testifying against his fellow bandits, and was subsequently released without charge. The detective who initially located Louis bought him a one-way ticket to Louis's hometown in Illinois and warned the robber against ever returning to California.

Eleanor slipped into Gilroy under the cover of darkness. She was too embarrassed and ashamed to admit to her friends and neighbors that she had married a thief. For anyone who dared ask what happened, she maintained that her mail-order groom had not been what she expected. Eventually, the truth of the ordeal became public knowledge and Eleanor was the topic of conversation. Humiliated beyond words, the young woman decided to commit suicide.

The distraught mail-order bride's life was saved by the fast action of her guardian and local doctors. It is not known what became of Eleanor after she was revived and brought back to health. Historians speculate that her broken heart mended and that true love eventually made her forget her first trip to the altar.

ASA MERCER
Bride Entrepreneur

*It is to the efforts of Mr. Mercer—joined with the wishes of
the darlings themselves—that the eleven accomplished and
beautiful young ladies whose arrival was recently
announced, have been added to our population.*

Seattle Gazette, 1864

In the February 24, 1860, edition of the *Puget Sound Herald*, an advertisement was published that testified to a serious shortage of a desired commodity in Washington Territory:

> ATTENTION BACHELORS: Believing that our only chance for the realization of the benefits and early attainment of matrimonial alliances depends on the arrival in our midst of a number of the fair sex from the Atlantic States, and that, to bring about such an arrival a united effort and action are called for on our part, we respectfully request a full attendance of all eligible and sincerely desirous bachelors of this community assemble on Tuesday evening next, February 28th, in Delim and Shorey's building, to devise ways and

Asa Mercer

means to secure this much-needed and desirable emigration to our shores.

Signed by nine leading citizens, the advertisement was picked up by other newspapers and reprinted across the country. Some of the resulting stories were humorous, but the wide coverage achieved the intent of the authors in broadcasting their need. They had hopes of attracting industrious young women to the rich and rugged Northwest, where a few thousand young men were working on making fortunes in timber, fishing, farming, and other endeavors. The lonely bachelors held several more meetings, but no solid plan to import the desired commodity was formulated, and few suitable women emigrated in response to the advertisement.

The pioneers in Washington Territory had, by 1860, established prosperous communities along Puget Sound and were busy carving out farms and ranches along the coast and toward the foothills of the Cascades. The temperate climate, rich fisheries, and timber resources provided the raw materials upon which to build a comfortable life. The one serious deficiency in this western Eden was that the "fair daughters of Eve" (as one newspaper editor described women) were scarce.

The topic had occupied many column inches in newspapers for several years. "There is probably no community in the Union of a like number of inhabitants in which so large a proportion are bachelors. We have no spinsters," wrote the editor of the *Puget Sound Herald*. He went on to say that the prosperous and clean-living young men populating the area in 1858 were "eager to put their necks in the matrimonial noose."

In 1860, Asa Shinn Mercer hit upon a scheme to take the next step in the recruitment effort: He would import the desired commodity by traveling to the East Coast, where women were in abundance, and actively promoting the unequaled advantages of Washington Territory. That idea and its sequel were part of the fascinating career of A. S. Mercer, who found his own bride among those he recruited for Washington Territory.

Fresh from college when he followed his older brother, popular Seattle pioneer Judge Thomas Mercer, to the Northwest, Asa slipped right into place in the ambitious new town. Asa worked enthusiastically to help erect a college, and he became a teacher at the Territorial University when it opened in 1861. He also served as the unofficial acting president when the first man recruited turned down the job, and he helped to recruit new students who could afford to pay the fees, which became part of his compensation.

The lack of marriageable women had become a serious detriment to progress. What good was a university if there were no wives to produce the sons to populate its halls? Seeing an unfilled need, Asa rushed to the rescue. He solicited private contributions to make a trip to the East Coast, and raised enough money to go to New England in 1863, with the hope of bringing back several hundred suitable ladies.

Unfortunately, a special committee had been appointed by the Massachusetts legislature to investigate the excess of females over males in that state, "amounting, according to the census of 1860, to 37,515." The committee had examined the state's needs for laborers in manufacturing businesses. Fearing that the end of the Civil War would see textile mills reopening, the report discouraged "any project from sending the surplus female population to such Western States as have an excess of males."

Asa hoped to attract hundreds of people, mostly marriageable women, but he was doomed to disappointment. As a result of his efforts, eleven unattached women paid $225 for passage and boarded the S.S. *Illinois* when it headed out to sea in the spring of 1864 on that "maiden voyage." The women were welcomed to Seattle, and all but two found husbands. Lizzie Ordway, who never married, was devoted to teaching and eventually became a county school superintendent. Another of the young ladies died, apparently of heart trouble.

Capitalizing on the buzz generated by his success, small though it was, Asa ran for a seat on the territory's governing council. In May 1864, the *Seattle Gazette* enthusiastically endorsed his candidacy.

Mr. Mercer is the Union candidate for joint councilman for King and Kitsap counties, and all such bachelors, old and young, may, on election day, have an opportunity of expressing, through the ballot box, their appreciation of his devotedness to the cause of the Union, matrimonial as well as national.

He won the seat, and served in the Territorial Legislative Assembly through January 1865. Then he undertook another recruiting expedition to the East. "One of the most enthusiastic supporters of my contemplated 'raid on the widows and orphans of the East,' as he was wont to call it, was

Governor William Pickering," Asa later recalled.

The day before I started for New York the governor met me, shook my hand warmly, and said: "God bless you, Mercer, and make your undertaking a great success. If you get into financial trouble and need money, do not hesitate to wire me and I will give you help."

A few months after arriving, Asa sent a letter to the folks back home from Lowell, Massachusetts. It was printed in the *Gazette,* and announced:

The 19th of August I sail from New York with upwards of three hundred war orphans—daughters of those brave, heroic sons of liberty, whose lives were given as offerings to appease the angry god of battle on many a plain and field in our recent war to perpetuate freedom and her institutions.

Asa asked the citizens of Seattle to prepare to house and care for the young ladies. He vouched for their intelligence and moral character. The papers reprinted his letter and communities immediately appointed welcoming committees, though some were dismayed at the number of women headed for their shores.

While the welcoming committees back home were meeting, Asa was running into rough waters. The *New York Times* endorsed the plan to ship widows and orphans to the new territory, and that sent would-be emigrants to Asa's door. But others sounded dire warnings that Asa was a procurer for the dens of iniquity in the West, and cautioned that those who left the safety of their families and their communities would suffer unmentionable fates.

Newspapers weighed in on the topic all across the country. The "surplus sweetness of Massachusetts spinsterhood" would be wasted in Washington Territory, opined the *LaCrosse Democrat.* The editorial continued:

Dr. Mercer has arrived in Boston and perfected arrangements to return at once with a cargo of Bay State Virgins, in black stockings, candlewick garters, shirt waists, spit curls, green specs, false teeth and a thirst for chewing gum.

Meanwhile, a famous female lecturer, Anna Dickinson, made biting remarks about the scheme, pointing out the odd logic involved in bringing schoolteachers to Washington Territory when it was common knowledge that the northern regions were populated largely by single men. "How your Washington bachelors can be fathers is a subject rather for a hearty guffaw than for any serious debate," Dickinson pointed out in an article reprinted in the *Alta California*. Her lectures in New England during the fall and winter of 1865 were widely attended and given a good deal of press coverage, which may have reduced the number of people interested in emigrating.

While the newspapers capitalized on the sensational aspects of the plan, Asa's capital was shrinking at an alarming rate. As Seattle historian Clarence Bagley later reported, "He was ever prone to take whatever he urgently hoped for as certain of accomplishment." Asa's urgently-hoped-for voyage with hundreds of accomplished young women and families, however, was almost stopped on the docks of New York.

The ship that Asa said was to have been made available by the federal government ended up in the hands of another schemer, who demanded a large sum to carry each of the passengers. The money he'd been given by young bachelors to cover costs of bringing back wives was long gone. Funds provided by others to be used for various investments had also been spent.

The delays, the loss of the ship, and finally, the negative publicity caused many of the young ladies and their families to cancel plans to join the expedition.

Five months late and several hundred ladies short, the S.S. *Continental* steamed out of New York Harbor January 16, 1866. Roger Conant, a New York reporter who traveled with the party, reported on the voyage. The departure was marred, says Conant, whose account was supported by several passengers, when some of those who had been promised passage were sent back before the ship left the harbor. Conant's version of events, as related in his journal, tells of an old man with five children being escorted off the ship when he could not pay the passage. The man's money had been used to cover hotel costs during the long delay.

Conant described the departure as though it were a theatrical farce:

The disappointed virgins screamed "Mr. Mercer! Mr. Mercer!!" The gray haired man hoarsely shouted "Mr. Mercer! Mr. Mercer!!" But no Mr. Mercer answered their appeals, and a thorough search of all the state rooms failed to discover his place of concealment.

Finally, the ticket-less would-be emigrants were escorted from the ship and the *Continental* edged out of the harbor.

Where was the hero of the day? Mercer was hiding in the coal bin. Conant describes the removal of the hatch cover once the ship was under way:

A heavy lumbering tread from below heralded the approach of the great benefactor of the virgin race. Soon a shock of red hair besprinkled with coal dust, bearing a strong resemblance to a zebra's skin, appeared below the opening. Then a pair of red eyes lifted themselves to the light. And soon a pair of hands were thrown upward in an appealing manner.

Mercer was lifted from his hiding place by a couple of sailors.

Flora Engle, who was fifteen at the time and traveling with her mother and brother to join her father and sister in Seattle, later wrote a long account of the voyage. Both Conant and Flora said that Mercer paid court to one young lady, but was rebuffed. "Mr. Mercer, who had formed a second attachment and had been so fortunate as to have his passion reciprocated, married Miss Annie Stephens of Baltimore," Flora reported. Annie's father owned a hat factory in Philadelphia. She and Asa were the same age—twenty-six—and though she was Catholic and he Methodist, they were married in Seattle in July 1866.

The ship arrived in San Francisco Bay on April 24, 1866. Some of the passengers, apparently daunted by dismal descriptions of the Pacific Northwest, decided to stay in sunny California. Obligated to pay the fare to Seattle for his remaining passengers, but with only a few dollars in his pocket, Asa sent an urgent request for money to the governor. He later recalled:

I spent $2.50 sending him a telegram: "Arrived here broke. Send $2,000 quick to get party to Seattle." The next day I received a notice from the telegraph office to call, pay $7.50 and receive a dispatch waiting for me. Having but 50 cents, I could not buy the message.

He went to the telegraph office, explained his penniless state to the superintendent, and suggested the man open the dispatch to see if it contained an order for money, which would allow him to pay. "He opened the envelope and read, then burst into a hearty laugh, and passed the message to me. It was made up of over 100 words of congratulation, but never a word about money."

Thirty-six passengers left the ship and stayed in California, but the rest took passage on various ships heading to Seattle, where, according to Flora Pearson:

Seattle housewives received them with open arms and vied with one another in entertaining the newcomers in their humble homes. And the men, well, they would fain open their arms also had they dared to do so. As it was, there was "standing room only" at some of the windows.

The Mercer Maids, as they came to be called, found husbands and jobs in Washington, Oregon, and California. Only a few returned to the eastern seaboard.

Asa, with his Irish bride behind him, embarked on a series of promotional and career adventures that sent them from place to place all over the West. He authored a forty-page pamphlet, *The Washington Territory: The Great Northwest, Her Material Resources and Claims to Emigration,* which was the first of many tracts promoting the Northwest. Relocating to Oregon, he became a customs collector in Astoria, where he was accused of smuggling. The matter was eventually discharged following unsuccessful attempts to prosecute the case. He then became involved in shipping and real estate. It was in Oregon that he again displayed his knack for promotion and began writing for newspapers.

By the 1880s Asa, Annie, and their children were living in Texas, where he founded and edited several publications. Moving to Wyoming, he started the *Northwestern Livestock Journal* and was involved with the Wyoming Stock Growers Association.

Annie died in 1900. She had given birth to eight children, three of whom died in infancy and one as a teenager. She had followed her husband from place to place, never complaining publicly about his enthusiastic promotions and the failures and public criticism that seemed to follow almost everything he did. Asa died at his home in the Big Horn Mountains in 1917. Though his schemes and dreams may have been bigger than the means to properly carry them out, his activities add a richly colored thread to the tapestry of western history.

MATRIMONIAL NEWS

*I*n the early days of westward travel, when men and women left behind their homes and acquaintances in search of wealth and happiness, there was a recognized need for some method of honorable introduction between the sexes. This need was readily fulfilled by the formation of a periodical devoted entirely to the advancement of marriage. Throughout the 1870s, '80s and '90s, that periodical, to which many unattached men and women subscribed, was a newspaper called *Matrimonial News.* The paper was printed in San Francisco, California, and Kansas City, Missouri. It was issued once a week and the paper's editors proclaimed that the intent of the material was the happiness of its readers.

According to the *Matrimonial News* business manager, Stark Taylor, the paper would "bring letters from a special someone to desiring subscribers in hopes that a match would be made and the pair would spend the rest of their life together."

Fair and gentle reader, can we be useful to you? Are you a stranger desiring a helpmate or searching for agreeable company that may in the end ripen into closer ties? If so, send us a few lines making known your desires. Are you bashful and dread publicity? Be not afraid. You need not disclose to us your identity. Send along your correspondence accompanied by five cents for every seven words, and we will publish it under an alias and bring about correspondence in the most delicate fashion. To cultivate the noble aim of life and help men and women into a state of bliss is our aim.

H. A. Repson, EXTRA FINISH   508 S. BROADWAY·
BALTIMORE, MD.

Unidentified mail-order bride poses for a photograph of the momentous day.

A code of rules and regulations, posted in each edition of the paper, was strictly enforced. All advertisers were required to provide information on their personal appearance, height, weight, and their financial and social positions, along with a general description of the kind of persons with whom they desired correspondence. Gentlemen's personals of forty words or under were published once for twenty-five cents in stamps or postage. Ladies' personals of forty words or under were published free of charge. Any advertisements over forty words, whether for ladies or gentlemen, were charged a rate of one cent for each word.

The personal ads were numbered, to avoid publishing names and addresses. Replies to personals were to be sent to the *Matrimonial News* office sealed in an envelope with the number of the ad on the outside.

Every edition of the *Matrimonial News* began with the same positive affirmation: "Women need a man's strong arm to support her in life's struggle, and men need a woman's love."

The following are a sample of advertisements that appeared in the January 8, 1887, edition of the Kansas City printing of *Matrimonial News*.

———— •◆• ————

283 - A gentleman of 25 years old, 5 feet 3 inches, doing a good business in the city, desires the acquaintance of a young, intelligent and refined lady possessed of some means, of a loving disposition from 18 to 23, and one who could make home a paradise.

———— •◆• ————

287 - An intelligent young fellow of 22 years, 6 feet height, weight 170 pounds. Would like to correspond with a lady from 18 to 22. Will exchange photos: object, fun and amusement, and perhaps when acquainted, if suitable, matrimony.

———— •◆• ————

...charge. All words over forty words, whether for ladies or gentlemen, will be charged for at the rate of one cent for each word. Ladies may answer as many as they please free of charge. All we ask ladies to do is to stamp each letter sent us to be forwarded.

5. A charge of ten cents in stamps for each letter sent to be forwarded to ladies must accompany the letters, but gentlemen answering three letters and enclosing thirty cents in stamps or postal order will be entitled to a free personal in the next issue. Therefore enclose your ad. with the letters and stamps.

Address all communications to the MATRIMONIAL NEWS, Room 8, Nos. 911 to 915, Main street, Kansas City, Mo.

lives in Kansas, 45 years old, height 5 feet, weight 220 pounds, brunette, black hair and eyes, wishes to correspond with ladies of suitable age, without incumbrance and with means, must move in the best society and be fully qualified to help make a happy home; object, matrimony. Full particulars must accompany first letter; send photo if convenient; all letters answered or returned.

286.—Am a lawyer, 30 years old, light complected, dark hair, 5 feet 10 inches tall, weight 150 pounds, would like to correspond with a good looking lady of some means; object, matrimony; photos exchanged.

287.—An intelligent young fellow of 22 years, 6 feet high, weight 170 pounds, would like to correspond with a lady from 18 to 22; will exchange photos; object, fun and amusement, and perhaps when acquainted, if suitable, matrimony.

Ladies.

Letters sent us by gentlemen to forward to ladies advertising will cost ten cents for each letter.

288.—I am a widow of 36 years, height 5 feet, weight 100 pounds, brunette, and wish to correspond with an honorable gentleman of suitable age; friendship and perhaps matrimony.

289.—I am 18, 5 feet 5 inches high, weight 140 lbs., auburn hair, dark brown eyes, full; I want a number of gentlemen correspondents, from 19 to 25. Object, let the future take care of itself.

290.—I am a jolly little widow, 34, neat and loving, brown hair, good reputation; would like to correspond with gentleman of means, neat and genteel, uses no liquor, of a kind heart, good reputation, must not be over 40. Please answer. Object, loving husband.

291.—A retired widow, small brunette of 30, reduced from affluence, desires to correspond with single gentleman of culture and refinement, some years her senior; enclose stamp for reply.

292.—Answer to No. 237.

FOUND.

A girl who will love,
Honest, true and not sour;
A nice little cooing dove,
And willing to work in flour.

293.—A beautiful little blonde of 16, weight 108 pounds, height 5 feet, desires to correspond with a gentleman of the opposite type; must be honorable, intelligent, and of stylish appearance, age 19 to 25, height 5 feet 8 inches, weight 145 to 175. Object made known through letter.

294.—A brunette of medium size, 5 feet 3 inches tall, would like to correspond with a good-hearted stockman, with a view to pleasant correspondence and perhaps matrimony.

295.—A jolly girl of 18 years, brown hair and eyes that are a bluish gray, and a fondness for fun and correspondence prompts to ask for gentlemen correspondents. Photo exchanged.

296.—A lady of nineteen, of highest character, educated and accomplished, would like to correspond with a gentleman of culture, not over 25. Object, pastime and possibly matrimony. Will exchange references and photos.

297.—Gentlemen: I am a brunette of 16 summers, gray eyes, height 5 feet, weight 115 pounds, and wish to correspond with an honorable gentleman of 19 to 25, a good housekeeper. Object, amusement and perhaps matrimony.

274.—An educated young lady of 23 years, light complexion, of medium size, domestic, good musician, would like to correspond with a gentleman of suitable age and of good character. Object, friendship and perhaps —.

275.—A young lady earning her own living, 24 years of age, 5 feet 5 inches tall, weight 126 pounds, good form, native of Missouri, desires correspondence with a view to matrimony. Photos exchanged.

276.—I am a brunette of 18 years, rather small, lively disposition, full of fun; would like to correspond with gent of culture. Object, good time.

277.—A maiden lady, nearly middle-aged, fair complexion, blue eyes, would be pleased to correspond with a gentleman of intelligence and culture and possessed of some means; a widower preferred.

238.—A stylish and accomplished young lady, in good standing, but lively and full of fun, wishes to correspond with a gentleman in high standing and who moves up the best society; one who can write a dandy letter strikes me with great force. I am 18 years old, have golden hair, blue eyes, a regular blonde, 5 feet 4 inches and weigh 130 pounds. Object, fun and the result. All letters promptly answered; photos exchanged.

239.—A highly respected and cultured young lady solicits correspondence with an honorable gentleman not over 35 years, of good standing, one who is full of fun and can write a jovial, good letter. I am 20 years of age, 5 feet 4 inches, weigh 125 pounds, dark hair and deep blue eyes, and of a lively disposition. As to "beauty," photo will speak. Object, fun, and if the harvest is love so much the better. All letters promptly answered; photos exchanged.

240.—I am a widow, dark hair, gray eyes, small but neat, 42 years old; would like to correspond with a business gentleman in

hear from some gentleman, widower preferred, between the age of 45 and 60, with a good home; I am a first-class housekeeper.

223.—I am a good looking, 19 years of age, have light hair and blue eyes, tall and of good form, desire the acquaintance of a nice gentleman who is good company. Object, companionship and matrimony after awhile.

224.—A widow of 32, dark hair and hazel eyes, highly cultured, weighing 150 pounds, 5 feet 3 inches tall, would like to find a good, kind husband.

225.—I am fond of fun, am 18, height 5 feet 5 inches, weight 140 pounds, have auburn hair, dark eyes; I want a gentleman correspondent, from 20 to 25. Object, fun and perhaps matrimony if suited.

226.—I am a jolly little girl of 17, with black hair and eyes, and fair complexion, weigh 115 pounds, am fond of company and would like to form the acquaintance of a nice gentleman or two, with whom I could spend an occasional evening socially, and if mutually agreeable, become friends, with proclivities tending ultimately to the greatest ambition of women.

227.—A jolly young lady, highly cultured, verging on 30, about 5 feet 4 inches in height and 140 pounds in weight, an extreme blonde, desires to correspond with a gentleman of sterling character, about 40 years of age. Would prefer a member of the Masonic fraternity who resides in the East, South or California.

228.—If there is a gentleman of honor and intelligence between the ages of 35 and 50 who wants a genuine housekeeper, let him write to this number. I am a widow, 38 years old, weigh 110 lbs., 5 feet 6 inches in height; am a brunette and have very fine black hair.

229.—I am an American widow, aged 50, 5 feet 1 inch in height, weight 127 lbs., a blonde, good form, intelligent, attractive and in good society, enjoying good health, am self sustaining, unincumbered and wish to correspond with gentleman of honor and suitable age.

230.—A young brunette of 19, refined and genteel and in business for myself, would like to correspond with a gentleman of character. Object, let the future take care of itself.

192.—A young Canadian lady, aged 26, brunette, large eyes, blue grey, hair black, height 5 feet 6 inches, accomplished, musical, thorough housekeeper, well connected. Gentleman answering this must be men of honor—that with me is more important than riches—bo tall, good-looking and refined and in every sense of the word a gentleman. I have no use for one who uses strong drink or chews that vile weed tobacco.

194.—I am a brunette of 19, weighing 132 pounds, height 5 feet 1 inch, pretty form, native of Indiana, of good family, love fun and home. Will exchange letters and photo with honorable gentleman.

195.—I am a blonde of 22 years, have brown hair and blue eyes, weigh 143 pounds, 5 feet and ½ inch high, round face, neat and tidy, fond of music. Want to correspond with a dark gentleman of character. Object, amusement and —.

196.—A cultured young lady of 19, medium height, dark hair, brown eyes, considered very good looking, jolly, of good family. Correspondence with gentlemen of means only desired. Photos exchanged.

197.—I am a blonde of 17, weigh 128 pounds, fair complexion, golden hair, violet blue eyes, height 5 feet 2 inches, accomplished in music and painting, wish to correspond with a tall, dark gentleman of temperate habits; object amusement and matrimony; photos exchanged.

198.—I am a widow 32 years of age, 5 feet 5 inches high, weigh 140 pounds, fair complexion, brown eyes and dark hair, would like to get acquainted with gentleman under 50; well, perhaps a pleasant acquaintance.

199.—I jolly widow of 30, height 5 feet 7 inches, weight 135 pounds, dark gray eyes, brown hair; would like a husband who would try to be a kind one.

200.—I am a brunette, have large black eyes and dark hair, fair complexion, am often taken for a Jewess, but I am not. Am bright and intelligent and love home. Am 19 years of age and would like to correspond with a kind hearted gentleman who can support a good wife.

201.—A young lady of 19 summers, height 5 feet 4 inches, weight 105 pounds, dark hair, gray eyes, of a loving disposition, a good housekeeper and also a lover of honor, would like a few gentlemen correspondents for pastime.

202.—I am a widow 23 years of age, weigh 145 pounds, of good form, walk erect, blue eyes and black hair; am self sustaining and independent. I would be pleased to correspond with a gentleman of suitable age who would like a companion of this class and who means business.

203.—I am 23 summers, 5 feet 4 inches high, wear No. 5 shoes and No. 6 glove, brown hair, gray eyes, cheerful, loving disposition, am

Men and women in hopes of finding a companion placed advertisements in a publication specifically designed for lonely hearts.

282 - A few lady correspondents wanted by a bashful man of 36, of fair complexion. 5 feet 5 inches tall, weight 130 pounds. Would prefer a brunette of fair form about five feet, between 18 and 25 years of age. Object, improvement, and if suited, matrimony.

——— ·◆· ———

278 - Wanted to correspond with a young lady matrimonially inclined who would make a young man a good wife: am of good standing and good family, strictly temperate, a professional man and will make a kind husband.

——— ·◆· ———

280 - A lively widower of 40, looking much younger, 5 feet 7 inches high, weighing 145 pounds would like to correspond with some maiden or widow lady of honor who would like a good home, kind husband and plenty.

——— ·◆· ———

281 - A miller by trade having some means strictly temperate. 30 years old, brunette would like to correspond with a good-looking lady of some means; object matrimony.

——— ·◆· ———

225 - I am fond of fun, age 18, height 5 feet 5 inches, weight 140 pounds, have auburn hair, dark eyes; I want a gentleman correspondent, from 20 to 25.

An unidentified mail-order bride submitted this photograph to the Kansas City edition of the Matrimonial News *in 1890.*

Object, fun and perhaps matrimony if suited.

———— .◆. ————

221 - A widow of 28. 5 feet 2 inches tall, black eyes and hair, weighing 125 pounds, wishes to make the acquaintance of some dark complexioned gentlemen of 25 to 45; am a first rate housekeeper.

———— .◆. ————

245 - I am fat, fair, and 48, 5 feet high. Am a No. 1 lady, well fixed with no encumbrance: am in business in city, but

The Kansas City edition of the Matrimonial News *published photographs of prospective brides like this young woman.*

want a partner who lives in the West. Want an energetic man that has some means, not under 40 years of age and weight not less than 180. Of good habits. A Christian gentlemen preferred.

———— •◆• ————

241 - I am a widow, aged 28, have one child, height 64 inches, blue eyes, weight 125 pounds, loving disposition. I am poor; would like to hear from honorable men from 30 to 40 years of old: working men preferred.

———— •◆• ————

NOTICE!

Due to the influx of Eastern "mail-order brides" into our community & the hasty marriages that follow, several complaints have been lodged by no-longer happy grooms.

THEREFORE

Let it be known that any marriage into which a man is seduced by the use of

- FALSE HAIR
- COSMETIC PAINTS
- ARTIFICIAL BOSOMS
- BOLSTERED HIPS
- PADDED LIMBS

without the man's knowledge, shall stand null & void if he so desires.

—JUDGE JOHN H. ARBUCKLE
Dated April 3, 1873

DO NOT BE DECEIVED

This warning appeared as an insert in several editions of the Matrimonial News *in the 1870s.*

228 - If there is a gentlemen of honor and intelligence between the ages of 35 and 50 who wants a genuine housekeeper, let him write to this number. I am a widow, 34 years old, weight 110 pounds, 4 feet and 5 inches in height: am brunette and have very fine black hair.

———— •◆• ————

292 - A girl who will love, honest, true and not sour; a nice little cooing dove, and willing to work in flour.

———— •◆• ————

It is estimated that in the three decades the paper was in existence more than 2,600 couples who advertised with the newspaper corresponded, exchanged photos, and eventually married.

PHOEBE HARRINGTON & WILLIAM SILBAUGH
The Hopeful Bride and the Farmer

William Silbaugh stopped to examine his reflection in a mercantile window. He smoothed his hair back and ran a finger over his bushy mustache. Confident that he looked presentable, he brushed down the wrinkles in his brown tweed suit and headed toward the train depot. The streets of Shoshone, Idaho, in 1911 were teeming with people going to work, shopping, and hurrying off to school. Lost in thought and feeling a bit anxious, William looked past his bustling surroundings and toward his future a few hundreds yards away, where the eastern bride he had ordered would be arriving on the afternoon train. Before the day was over, he would be a married man.

William Henry Silbaugh was born and raised around Bruceton Mills, West Virginia. Poor health, however, drove him to a drier climate, and he settled in Idaho in 1906, where he was employed as a surveyor of town sites in various parts of the state. While reviewing the thoroughfares of Jerome, Idaho, he decided he needed a wife. He asked his aunt in West Virginia to shop for a woman for him, and to send the candidate on once she met with her approval.

Armed only with a written description of his mail-order bride, he scanned the faces of the passengers staring out the train, as it slowed to a stop. He recognized his wife-to-be as she stepped out of the car and onto the depot walkway. Phoebe Harrington was a seventeen-year-old woman with a tiny waist and a petite frame. The two exchanged pleasantries, collected her bags, and then walked down the street to the justice of the peace.

William and Phoebe had known each other less than an hour when they exchanged vows. After the quick ceremony, William helped his bride into a buckboard and escorted her to his farm twenty miles away.

Phoebe drank in the scenery as they made their way to Appleton, Idaho. The landscape was substantially different from the area of Pennsylvania from which she hailed. She believed the move West was necessary for her to improve her life's standing. She was one of six children in her family, and her mother had died when Phoebe was eleven years old. Shortly thereafter she went to work as a domestic servant to help support her brothers and sisters. After sixteen years working as a maid, she was presented with an opportunity she hoped would improve her situation. She responded to an advertisement for a wife and was selected to travel to Idaho to marry a twenty-year-old farmer with land and promise.

The homestead William owned was located in Magic Valley. It was his belief—as well as that of other area farmers—that the rich, virgin soil would produce healthy crops of wheat, potatoes, alfalfa, beans, peaches, and apples. The fields had yet to be plowed, but Phoebe could imagine their potential as William described how the landscape would look.

The Silbaughs set up house in a small, windowless, two-room shack north of the Snake River. When Phoebe wasn't busy cooking, sewing, and cleaning, she worked in her garden and helped William keep the crops irrigated. In addition to maintaining the farm, William cared for a herd of sheep. The sheep sustained the Silbaughs during the time they struggled to grow their crops. In spite of the euphoric name given to the valley, and all the newlyweds' efforts, the land would not yield quality produce.

Hope for the Silbaughs' forty acres began to dwindle, but their family grew. Nine months after the young couple was married, Phoebe gave birth to the first of their seven children. After twenty-five years of struggling to make the farm a minor success, William decided to move his wife and children north to a ranch near the town of Salmon.

The Silbaughs' fourteen-acre spread rested on Fourth of July Creek. There was plenty of water for crops and pasture for the sheep. In a short time, Phoebe and the Silbaugh family were living the life William had dreamed of providing for them.

In 1958, William and his mail-order bride celebrated forty-seven years of marriage. Their time together ended when William was killed in a car accident. Phoebe died sixteen years later of heart failure at eighty-one years old.

THE FORLORN BRIDE

A brassy sun was beginning to lengthen the morning shadows when Mary Zadow raced out of her parents' home, gasping for breath. Her pretty face was pale and strands of her long, dark, curly hair clung to the sweat on her cheeks and neck. Her eyes were swollen with tears as she dropped to her knees and clutched her chest. Mary's mother, Ester, was standing on the neighbor's porch when she saw her daughter collapse. She hurried over to her child and fell down beside her. "I told you I would do it," Mary gasped. "I told you!" Ester brushed the fifteen-year-old girl's hair out of her face and laid her down in the grass. Mary's eyes closed.

"Hurry!" Ester shouted to her neighbor friend who was watching the incident curiously. "Bring me a mustard and vinegar mixture! Please hurry!" The frantic mother gently shook her daughter, and Mary's eyes gradually opened. "It's no use," Mary told Ester. "I'm dying." Tears burst from Ester's eyes and she shook her daughter again as she called out for the neighbor to hurry along. "Goodbye," Mary said softly. She exhaled one last time and then passed from this life. Ester wept bitterly as she rocked her child's body back and forth.

Citizens around the Zadow residence in the mining town of Iowa Hill emerged from their homes to see what all the commotion was about. One by one they ventured over to the grieving mother. Their hearts broke as they watched Ester clutch Mary to her breast.

When the Zadows ventured west from Ohio in 1863, they imagined a prosperous life in California for themselves and their three children. It was Mary who finally convinced her parents to move from their farm and try their hands at gold mining. She read newspaper articles to her father, Albert, that described the Gold Country as "heaven on earth." The same articles boasted that fortunes could be made not only panning for gold but working the rich soil around the diggings. Albert reasoned that if he did not hit the mother lode, he could return to farming and provide pioneers with fruit and vegetables. Mary was elated about the move, but the source of her excitement had more to do with a young man than the adventures to be had crossing the plains.

Unbeknownst to either of her parents, Mary had been corresponding with a twenty-eight-year-old man named Calvin Howell. Calvin had placed an ad in the *Matrimonial News,* looking for a wife. He lived in the tiny mining town of Ophir, near Auburn, California, and had his own mining claim. According to his ad, he wanted "a sweet someone to share his earnings and future with." Mary responded to his advertisement and the two wrote to one another for three months before Calvin asked her to marry him. Neither Ester nor Albert could read so they believed Mary when she told them the letters she received were from one of her teachers who had moved to San Francisco.

Mary accepted Calvin's proposal, but decided to keep the engagement a secret until her family arrived in California. Her journal reads that she was "afraid her parents would object to their union because of her young age." Mary believed that their hearts would soften once they met Calvin and saw how deeply they cared for one another.

Four days after the Zadows arrived in Iowa Hill, Calvin Howell came calling. Neither Mary nor Calvin was disappointed in how the other looked. On the contrary, both were instantly smitten and fell easily into conversation about the trip and the area.

Albert and Ester were not as impressed with Calvin. After confessing that the claim he had been working for more than a year had yielded only a small amount of gold, the Zadows decided he would ultimately not be able to provide their daughter with even the basic comforts. Calvin assured them that his claim would pay off eventually and that he would give Mary the world. Even if Calvin had been solvent, however, there was the matter of age difference. Mary was thirteen years younger than Calvin and her parents would not consent to the union. Mary pleaded and cried, but Albert remained steadfast in his decision. Calvin sadly left the Zadow home, fearing he would never see Mary again.

The Zadow family settled into the Iowa Hill community, going about their day-to-day business and believing that the notion of marrying Calvin Howell had been erased from Mary's thoughts. It had not. She pined for Calvin and reread his letters over and over. He did the same with her letters.

Several weeks after their first meeting, Calvin made another appeal to Albert and Ester. This time he brought a couple of local citizens with him to vouch for his honorable character. The Zadows again refused to let their daughter go. A longing glance passed between Calvin and Mary at that meeting, and in that look was the determination to do whatever it took to be together.

On a warm Sunday morning in August, two months after the Zadows arrived in California, the family prepared to attend church services. Mary pretended to be too ill to go along. She encouraged her parents and two brothers to leave her behind. Just as the family buggy disappeared from sight, Mary raced out the back door and hurried off to find Calvin.

Calvin saw Mary running up the gravel road towards his claim and he hurried out to meet her. The couple embraced and proclaimed their love for one another. It was the first of many secret rendezvous.

At home, Mary tried in vain to convince her mother and father to allow her to see Calvin, but they maintained their position. Mary threatened to kill herself if they wouldn't let her be with Calvin. They dismissed the warning as "overemotional hysterics" and sent her to her room.

During one of the couple's clandestine meetings, Mary told Calvin about a dog in the neighborhood that was bothering her.

"He's mean and I'm afraid he's going to bite me," she wrote in her journal about what she told Calvin. He informed her that "a pinch of arsenic is the best way to handle such a beast." And as promised, he provided her with a small bag of arsenic at their next visit.

"Why can't my folks see that I love him?" she noted in her journal. "I've got to make them see how much he means to me . . . or die trying," she vowed. No amount of talk or tears would change her parents' minds. "You're too young," they insisted.

On the day Mary felt she had no choice but to take her own life, she watched her mother head out the front door and cross over to the neighbors' home. With tears streaming down her face, she poured half the arsenic Calvin had given her into a glass of water and drank the poison down.

The news of Mary's demise devastated Calvin. After attending her funeral, he locked himself inside his cabin near his claim. When his friends dropped by to check on him three days later, they found him dead. A mixture of water and arsenic was spilled next to Calvin's body. Nearby, the note he left behind revealed what had happened. "I'm sorry," the note read. "But I've gone to be with Mary."

BETHENIA OWENS-ADAIR & LEGRAND HILL
The Doctor and the Farmer

On May 4th, with only our old friends, the Perrys, and the
minister present, beside our own family, we were married. I was
still small for my age. My husband was five-feet eleven inches in
height, and I could stand under his outstretched arm.

Bethenia Owens-Adair—1854

ifteen-year-old Bethenia Owens-Hill stared out the window of her husband's aunt's farmhouse, rocking her infant son to sleep. A brisk wind pelted the glass with sand and dust. Drought-twisted sagebrush tumbled past her bleak, hazy view and continued on. Bethenia's baby whimpered a bit and she kissed his tiny forehead. Tears drifted down her face and she brushed them away with the back of her hand. Her Aunt Kelly entered the room from the kitchen and placed a pot of stew on a neatly set table. Bethenia turned away from her aunt, hoping she wouldn't be caught crying, but it was too late. The concerned woman gently walked over to her distressed niece and put a comforting arm around her.

"Now Bethenia," she said kindly, "You just give him to me. I'll take him, and educate him, and make him my heir. I'll give him all I have, and that's more than his father will ever do for him."

"My baby is too precious to give to anyone," Bethenia replied in a hurt voice. "You seem to think that will make things all right." The young mother sobbed into her child's blanket. Her aunt apologized and tried to persuade her to eat something. Bethenia declined, choosing instead to pace the floors with her baby boy.

When Bethenia's parents arranged for their daughter to marry Legrand Hill, a farmer who had advertised for a bride in the Oregon newspapers in February of 1854, they never imagined the union would turn out to be such an unhappy one and that Bethenia would be left to raise her son alone.

Bethenia Angelina Owens was one of nine children born to Thomas and Sarah Damron Owens in February 1840. When Bethenia was three, her father moved the family from Van Buren County, Missouri, to Clatsop, Oregon. The Owens crossed the plains with the first emigrant wagon trains of 1843. Thomas came west to acquire a large parcel of land the government had encouraged pioneers to claim on the new frontier. Settling at the mouth of the Columbia River, the Owens entered into the cattle ranching profession.

As the second oldest child in the family, Bethenia was given the job of babysitter for her younger brothers and sisters, while her mother and older sister helped work the ranch. According to her memoirs she often had one of her siblings in her arms and more clinging to her.

Where there is a baby every two years, there is always no end of nursing to be done; especially when mother's time is occupied, as it was then, every minute, from early morning till late at night, with much outdoor as well as indoor work. She [Bethenia's mother] *seldom found time to devote to the baby, except to give it the breast.*

Bethenia Owens-Adair—October 1906

Bethenia was barely fourteen when she first made the acquaintance of Legrand Hill. He had been living in the Rogue River Valley for a year and working his parents' land. He was a handsome man, broad-shouldered and tall. When she looked into his eyes, she saw the promise of a long and happy life. Her parents had selected this man to be her husband and she trusted their decision. On their recommendation she eagerly placed her future in Legrand's hands. On May 4, 1854, the petite teenager, dressed in a sky-blue wedding dress, stood next to her groom and promised to be a faithful wife.

Dr. Bethenia Owens-Adair

After the ceremony the pair retired to their home in the middle of 320 acres of farmland Legrand had purchased on credit. The newlyweds lived four miles from Bethenia's parents and in the beginning, all was right with the world. Family and friends visited often, helping Legrand work the property and assisting Bethenia as she made repairs to their small log cabin.

I had high hopes and great expectations for the future. My husband was a strong, healthy man; I had been trained to work, and bred to thrift and economize, and everything looked bright and beautiful to me. My soul overflowed with love and hope, and I could sing the dear old home-songs from morning to night.

Bethenia Owens-Adair—June 1854

Legrand was an avid hunter, and in between planting and tending to the livestock, he spent days in the forest bagging grouse and deer. Before long, Legrand's hunting trips became an obsession. More often than not, he put off doing chores to track wild game. He idled away so much time Bethenia's father was forced to complete the job of putting up a good winter house to protect his daughter from the elements. A mere nine months after their wedding, Bethenia had fully recognized in Legrand a "lack of industry and perseverance."

Legrand was opposed to doing an honest day's work and because of that, he was unable to pay the $150 mortgage on the farm. The Hills were forced to sell the land and move to Jackson County, Oregon, to live with Legrand's Aunt Kelly.

Less than a year after the Hills were married, Bethenia gave birth to a boy. The proud couple named the child George. Legrand's slothful ways, however, did not change with the advent of fatherhood. He continued to fritter away his time, leaving the responsibility of earning an income to Bethenia.

Mr. Hill neither drank or used tobacco, but, as his aunt said during one of my long stays with her, he simply idled away his time, doing a day's work here and there, but never continuing at anything. Then, too, he had a passion for trading and speculating, always himself coming out a loser.

Bethenia Owens-Adair—October 1906

Bethenia's parents paid the young mother a visit and were appalled by the "hand to mouth" living situation in which they found their daughter and grandchild. Thomas managed to persuade his son-in-law to return to Clatsop County. He lured the less than ambitious Legrand back with an offer to give him an acre of land and material to build a house.

To say that we were delighted with this proposal expresses it but faintly. We sold our house in Yreka, realizing less than $100 out of the transaction, as the $150 mortgage and interest had to come out of the sum received for the property, but father said, "A bird in the hand is worth two in the bush." We were soon packed and ready to start our migration.

Bethenia Owens-Adair—October 1906

Legrand's attitude toward work remained the same in Clatsop County. Against the advice of his father-in-law, he agreed to partner in a brick-making business. Legrand turned what little money he and Bethenia had over to his two partners and then spent all of his time overseeing the venture. He decided against building a home for his wife and child and chose instead to move his family into a tent. A sustained torrential downpour halted the making of the bricks and eventually put an end to the business altogether.

In late November, Bethenia contracted typhoid fever. She was much too sick to care for her baby or work to keep food on the Hill table. Her parents stepped in and moved Bethenia and George out of the damp tent and into their dry home.

Thomas pleaded with Legrand to start construction on a house for his family, but he refused to do so until the deed to the land was turned over to him. When Thomas refused to give in to his request, Legrand became furious and decided to build a house in town instead. He proved to be a poor carpenter and after four months. the home was still not complete. Wife and child were moved in anyway.

The kitchen was so open that the skunks, which were very numerous in that region at that time, came under the floor nights, and up into the kitchen, where they rattled around among the pots and pans, even jumping on the table, and devouring the food, if I did not keep everything securely covered, while I often lay and listened to their nocturnal antics, not daring to get up to drive them out, as the dire consequences of disturbing them suddenly were well known.

Bethenia Owens-Adair—October 1906

Bethenia continued to struggle with her health. The fever had left her weak and unable to do everything she once did. George was sickly too, but was nonetheless a big eater. Legrand had little or no patience with his three-year-old son's ailments. He spanked him quite frequently for whimpering, and in many instances, was generally abusive toward the toddler.

Early one morning in March, after a tempestuous scene of this sort, Mr. Hill threw the baby on the bed, and rushed downtown. As soon as he was out of sight, I put on my hat and shawl, and gathering a few necessaries together for the baby, I flew over to father's.

Bethenia Owens-Adair—October 1906

Sarah Owens applauded her daughter's courage in leaving Legrand. "Any man that could not make a living with the good starts and help he has had, never will make one," she told Bethenia. "And with his temper, he is

44

Le gouverneur de la Californie, après avoir vu partir tous ses domestiques pour les mines, se voit abandonné même par sa femme et par son fils.

French Advertisement, 1957. Owner of a home watches his female servant leave for California where women are worth their weight in gold.

liable to kill you at any time." Bethenia remained at her parents' home even though Legrand made numerous appeals to win her back. "I told him many times," she later wrote in her journal, "that if we ever did separate, I would never go back and I never will."

After four years of living in a difficult marriage, Bethenia filed for divorce. Many Clatsop County residents were shocked by her actions, and a family neighbor advised Bethenia to "go back and beg him on your knees to receive you." The forlorn mother refused. "I was never born to be stuck by mortal man," she insisted.

Although difficult at first, Bethenia and George's life away from Legrand and his tyrannical behavior proved to be best for mother and son. George thrived under his grandparents' roof, basking in the constant attention he received from his many aunts and uncles. Bethenia was coming into her own as well, deciding to go back to school and study medicine while holding down several jobs to support herself and her child. In 1861, she had saved enough money to purchase a plot of land in Astoria, Oregon, and build a house.

Legrand, who seemed to never have gotten over losing Bethenia, wrote her constantly during this time, pleading with her to remarry him. Refusing to accept her written refusal, he showed up on the doorstep of her new home, crying and begging for a second chance. "But alas for him," Bethenia wrote in her journal, "He found not the young, ignorant, inexperienced child-mother whom he had neglected and misused, but a full-grown, self-reliant woman who could look upon him only with pity."

Bethenia divided her time between her son, her education, and her work. Her fine business sense enabled her to make a substantial living as a milliner and dressmaker, and with the money she earned, she was able to send her son to college and on to medical school. After acquiring a loan to further her own education, Bethenia entered a school in Philadelphia where she graduated with a degree in hydropathy medicine—a form of alternative medicine based upon the principle that water is the most basic element and also the most important aspect to good health.

After receiving further medical training at schools in Michigan and Chicago, she returned to Clatsop County in 1883 and opened her own practice. She was the first woman doctor in the state of Oregon.

In 1884, she married Colonel John Adair, but her duties as a physician took precedence over her duties as a wife, and the pair eventually divorced. Bethenia practiced medicine until she was sixty-five.

What became of Legrand Hill, Bethenia's ex mail-order spouse, is unknown. Some Jackson County, Oregon, historians speculate that after Bethenia's final rejection he returned to his parents' home and drank himself to death.

THE BENTON BRIDES
Tales of a Trip to Matrimony

*I*n the mid-1860s, more than one hundred women from the small town of Ellicott City, Maryland, favorably responded to a mailed advertisement to become wives of bachelors in Oregon. Two of the adventurous ladies who agreed to make the trip kept journals of their mail-order bride travels. Their entries describe their motivation to marry, what they were willing to endure, and their zeal to bring stability to the unsettled West.

The hard, frost-covered ground cracked under Constance Ranney's fast-moving feet. She pulled a wool shawl tight around her shoulders and buried her face in her chest. The winter air blowing off the water and over the town of Ellicott City, Maryland, was frigid and sharp. But the weather was not slowing the attractive, twenty-year-old woman down. She lifted the hem of her long Gibson skirt out of the snow and walked with great purpose toward Town Hall.

Before entering the building, Constance unfolded a leaflet she had clutched tightly in her hand and reread the bold print. The words "Brides Wanted" were scrawled across the top. The advertisement, which had been mailed to every home in Ellicott City, encouraged marriageable women to consider sailing to Oregon's Willamette Valley to meet and marry the eligible bachelor of her choice. Interested ladies were asked to meet at Town Hall to learn more about the particulars of the trip.

It was December 1864 and the frontier beyond Kansas was sadly lacking in women. Drastic measures were being used by lonely pioneer men to entice single ladies from the East to relocate to the West. Women who considered making such a journey were promised security and happiness in a land rich with opportunity.

Constance refolded the leaflet and tucked it into her pocket. As she neared the meeting place, she noticed a few other women heading in the same direction. The Civil War had left an abundance of unmarried ladies in Ellicott City and the number of available males was slim. Many of these women reasoned, as Constance did, that this might be their best chance to avoid spinsterhood.

The women entered Town Hall and took a seat in the galley, speaking to one another in hushed tones, and comparing the leaflets they had received. Constance stood in the back of the room surveying the scene, debating whether or not to join the others. In a letter she wrote to her uncle after the meeting, she told him that her moment of indecision had been short-lived: "Such a challenge was being presented—to go to an uncivilized land and make it civilized. Then it struck me. If I don't do this I will spend my entire life working as a servant for the rich here."

Constance was employed as a personal maid to the daughter of one of the wealthiest men in Ellicott City. She disliked her job and the daughter in particular. According to her journal, the woman treated Constance badly. The notion of having to keep such a job was distressing to her, but alternatives in Maryland were limited. Constance sat down with the other women and waited for the meeting to start.

Archer Benton, a tall, well-built man with dark, unruly hair and a thick mustache made his way from a chair in front to a lectern. He was dressed in a brown suit, the jacket of which had obviously not been worn for some time, as the fit was a bit too snug. Even so, Constance noted that he "looked as if he possessed both brains and ambition."

All eyes were on Archer as he smiled at the crowd before him. After introducing himself—and his brothers Thadeus and Samuel, who were also present—he proceeded to explain to the eager audience his plan to take all interested parties to Oregon. The Bentons were owners of a sawmill in Albany, Oregon, and had been commissioned by the many eligible bachelors there to solicit brides.

Archer promised the ladies a peaceful, tree-filled terrain, endless blue skies, and a husband for every widow and spinster. At the conclusion of his talk, several hopeful ladies hurried to sign a contract agreeing to make the trip. Constance Ranney was among them.

Constance wrote her uncle that many of the girls at the meeting were from good families, "the kind of families that would never have me in their parlors because I'm a servant." She went on to explain, "In Oregon, we will all be the same, just women looking for husbands. None of us any better than the other."

Less than a week after the idea of such a trip had been presented, Constance and the one hundred-plus other women who agreed to accompany the Benton Brothers back to Oregon were packed and waiting at the dock. Women like Josephine Ann Gibney would make the journey with her parents' blessing. Constance's parents forbade her to go, but she went anyway.

On the morning of January 16, 1865, the Benton Brothers' bevy of mail-order brides boarded a schooner called the *Osceolo*. The accommodations aboard were primitive, but the excited women were too preoccupied—with the anticipation of what the future would bring—to mind. The hopeful brides exchanged tearful goodbyes with loved ones. Some of the women continued waving to their family members until the coastline faded from site.

It wasn't long after the ship set sail that the majority of passengers went below deck and saw for the first time the vessel's disorderly state. The boat was generally used to transport mules, and the ladies' quarters were nothing more than stalls. Some of the women were so appalled at the unsanitary conditions and the smell that they demanded the Bentons turn the ship around and take them home. Josephine Ann Gibney was one of a handful of ladies who tried to bring order to the offended women.

After much complaining and discussion about how the rugged West might be comparable and we'd be required to make the best of things there, we decided to press on. We tidied up the areas where we would be sleeping that night and determined to thoroughly clean our temporary home the next day.

J. A. Gibney—January 16, 1865

After several days of scrubbing and scouring, the women had transformed the mule scowl into a pristine, fresh-smelling freighter. Dispositions further improved when the ladies took over the kitchen. Once the galley had been fully cleaned, the ship's crew was relieved of all cooking duties.

I think everyone is happier now that things have been set to order and we've begun doing some cooking. I was able to help out quite a bit in this area, as I used to be a cook on my grandfather's ship. I set about to help organize the tasks and shifts as I understand how to cook for a large group of people at once.

J. A. Gibney—January 27, 1865

The spirits of the sailors working aboard the *Osceolo* were lifted by the changes made to the ship, in particular the quality of meals the women served. Some of the men commented that it was the "finest food offered up on the vessel since it was first set in the ocean."

The "brides," as the ship's crew referred to them, were not satisfied with simply improving the freighter cosmetically but sought to clean things up socially as well. They prohibited the crew from drinking alcohol, and demanded that they bathe regularly and observe the Sabbath along with them. At Archer Benton's strong urging, the sailors reluctantly agreed.

The ship's captain presided over the first Sunday service. He delivered a message about Moses leading the Israelites to the Promised Land. Although rough waters and seasickness kept many women away from the worship time, the sermon ended with a few ladies singing a traditional hymn.

For two weeks the schooner was violently tossed about by relentless waves, and more brides fell ill. Cold winter winds that whipped across the boughs kept them all below deck. Constance Ranney was one of the ladies who longed to relieve her suffering with a walk across the ship's deck.

Oh, to feel a breeze across my face, but I can barely raise my head to write this now. The uneasiness in my stomach makes it impossible to keep down any nourishment. There is a girl on the ship who is trying to help, but it appears all she can do is give out cold compresses for our heads and encourage us that this also will pass.

Constance Ranney—January 30, 1865

A Husband Wanted

By a Lady who can wash, cook, scour, sew, milk, spin, weave, hoe, (can't plow), cut wood, make fires, feed the pigs, raise the chickens, rock the cradle, (gold-rocker, I thank you sir!), saw a plank, drive nails, etc. These are few solid branches; now for the ornamental. "Long time ago" she went as far as syntax, read Murray's Geography and through rules in Pike's Grammor. Could find six states on the Atlas. Could read, and you can see she can write. Can—no, could paint roses, butterflies, ships, etc. Could once dance) can ride a horse, donkey or oxen, besides a great many things too numerous to be named bare. Oh, I bear you aks, could she scold? No, she can't you, you ____ ____. good-for-nothing!

Now for her terms. He age is none of your business. She is neither handsome nor a fright, yet an old man need not apply, nor any who have not a little more education than she has, and a great deal more guid, for there must be $20,000 settled on her before she will bind herself to perform all the above.

Advertisement placed by Dorothy Scaraggs, Marysville, California newspaper, April 1849.

The choppy waters upset Josephine Ann Gibney as well, but not because it made her nauseated. She had lost her grandfather and uncle when their fishing vessel capsized during a storm.

Not doing as well as yesterday. All this reminds me much too much of events from my past. I find that my hands are shaking and my breathing is quick. I hope this does not last much more, as I am not sure how long I'll be able to take feeling this frightened.

J. A. Gibney—January 30, 1865

Matrimonial News
San Francisco, CA
May 1873

A bachelor of 40, good appearance and substantial means, wants a wife. She must be under 30, amiable and musical.

————— •◆• —————

A lady, 23, tall, fair and good looking, without means, would like to hear from a gentleman of position wanting a wife. She is well educated, accomplished, amiable, and affectionate.

————— •◆• —————

Aged 27, height 4 feet 9 inches, dark hair and eyes, considered handsome by all his friends untied in saying his amiable and will make a model husband. The lady must be one in the most extended acception of the word since the advertiser moves in the most polished and refined society. It is also desirable that she should have considerable money.

————— •◆• —————

I am 33 years of age, and as regards looks can average with most men. I am looking for a lady to make her my wife, as I am heartily tired of bachelor life. I desire a lady not over 28 or 30 years of age, not ugly, well educated and musical. Nationality makes no difference, only I prefer not to have a lady of Irish birth. She must have at least $20,000.

————— •◆• —————

Young lady of good family and education would like to correspond with some gentleman of means, one who would be willing to take her without a dollar, as she has nothing to offer but herself.

The *Osceolo* traveled a southerly course toward its destination. The further south they went, the calmer the waters became. By the first week of February, nearly all the women had recovered and were enjoying long walks topside. Being able to take in a clear sunset and breathe the fresh air reinvigorated the brides. One evening crewmembers entertained the recuperating ladies with a musical program. A quartet of sailors sang while another member of the crew accompanied them on a mouth harp. Some of the women danced with the men, and afterward they were all treated to a meal of soup and crackers.

On Sunday, February 7, 1865, both passengers and crew congregated on the deck of the ship for Sabbath services. A strong wind again created big swells that pelted the sides of the vessel, but it did not detract from the worship time. One of the older brides-in-waiting gave the sermon and led the group in a hymn and closing prayer. All were hopeful that the hard times they'd encountered while en route to Oregon were over.

As Sunday morning turned to dusk, larger waves crashed against the ship's hull. The water and wind were so loud they overpowered one sailor's call for help. A crewman working near the ship's stern had lost his balance and fallen overboard. By the time his desperate cry was heard it was too late. Life preservers were tossed out, but they failed to reach the man before the strong ocean current swept him away.

Efforts to save the pitiful man did not work. I watched in horror as he drifted further and further out into the gray water and then vanished under a wave. It made us all realize how much we are at the mercy of the sea. May God have mercy on the man's soul.

Constance Ranney—February 8, 1865

A somber mood fell over the hearts of the surviving crewmembers and the women. The tragedy clouded the attitudes of the passengers and February passed slowly for them. By the middle of March, they were restless and anxious to reach the Oregon coast.

How much longer? My seasickness has been replaced by homesickness. I know that it will pass once I am on dry land and have the privilege of meeting the man who will take me as his wife. I can hardly wait another day!

Constance Ranney—March 16, 1865

On April 4, 1865, the *Osceolo* pulled into an Oregon port. More than 150 men, loggers, and miners from the Willamette Valley were on hand to greet the women.

The brides disembarked carrying letters of introduction in one hand and the single suitcase they had been permitted to bring in the other. The beautiful landscape was just as the Benton Brothers had described it. Snow-covered mountain peaks, dense forests, and clear water surrounded them and beckoned them on to their new lives.

The brides were happily escorted to the town of Albany. Within a year's time all but seven of the women had married. Constance Ranney's and Jospehine Ann Gibney's journals ended once they reached dry land. The written account of their travels from Maryland to Oregon has been preserved at the Maritime Museum in Portland.

A HAPPY RIDE

*A*n excerpt from a newspaper in Northern California describes a controversial event that took place at a gentlemen's club meeting in Nevada County. A group of prominent men, convinced that being single was better than being married, met on a regular basis to discuss the benefits of remaining unattached. The organization's commitment to that belief was challenged when one member dared to follow through with plans to marry his mail-order bride.

One of the many devious ways in which the course of true love can be made to run was illustrated in Grass Valley recently—showing how by a chance buggy ride, a man saved $2000 and gained a wife. A certain young bachelor of Grass Valley paid his "distresses" to one of the beautiful young ladies so numerous in this grassy vale, and matters were rapidly progressing towards a matrimonial entanglement, when for some reason best known to himself the wooing swain "flew the track." The deserted mail-order maiden was a girl of spirit, and she immediately commenced suit for breach of promise to marry. The trial commenced January 11, 1881, and the contest waxed hot for three days, resulting in a verdict for the fair plaintiff, with $2000 damages.

Consternation was carried into the camp of the bachelors by this threatening result. A meeting of the Bachelor's Club of Grass Valley was instantly called to discuss the situation and deliberate upon precautionary measures, to protect others of the fraternity from the fate that had overtaken their brother. Among other things it was proposed that all members who were in dangerous habit of calling upon marriageable ladies should supply themselves with a receipt book,

ESPECIALLY DEDICATED TO OUR LADY READERS IN THE EAST.

NEEDS NO COMMENT.

Miners published this cartoon to accompany a poem entitled "We Miss Thee, Ladies"—a proposal of marriage to missing women.

and have a release signed at the termination of each visit, stating that no matrimonial engagement had been entered into, and that all was square to date.

In an earnest speech and with a voice trembling with emotion, the president besought the members to specially avoid osculation, as in law a kiss was regarded as a seal to an implied contract making it binding upon the parties. The club adjourned without taking final action, and the members departed to their homes with a deep-rooted apprehension lurking in their bosoms, and resolved to spend their money on billiards and fast horses and let the girls severally alone.

And now comes the romantic termination. About three months later a heavily loaded stage was on its way from Nevada City to Grass Valley, when it was met by a gentleman in a buggy, who offered to relieve the stage of one of the passengers, provided the person was willing to return to Nevada City while he was transacting a little business. The innocent driver gazed down into the stage and asked a lady if she desired to accept the gentleman's offer.

She did desire and did accept, and alighted from the stage which immediately drove away. Then it was that the old-time lovers and recent litigants found that they were destined to take a ride. What was said during that ride we know not, but when they arrived in Nevada City, they went before Judge Reardon, the same who had presided at the trial, and were quickly made one. Indignant at this defection of a member whom they had considered their staunchest adherent, the Bachelor's Club called another meeting and expelled him with imposing ceremonies."

The *Daily Transcript*—May 10, 1881

RACHEL BELLA KAHN & ABRAHAM CALOF
Northern Plains Pioneer Couple

*T*he clump of yarn Rachel Bella Kahn was attempting to unravel was a mixture of complicated knots and tangles. The seventeen-year-old servant girl painstakingly worked through the mass of thick threads, rolling the straightened strands into a neat, tight ball. Chaya Calof, a graying, older woman from Chvedkifka, Russia, watched the young woman's every move closely. After several moments Rachel patiently and successfully transformed the snarled ball into a manageable skein.

The ball of yarn was politely handed over to Chaya, who grinned from ear to ear. "Good," she told her, "Good. You've passed the test." The teenager breathed a sigh of relief. Chaya's approval was all that was standing in the way of Rachel's marriage to the North Dakota farmer seeking her hand.

"A wife of good, strong character is what I seek, but it is optional. To be of the Jewish faith is mandatory," wrote Abraham Calof in 1892. Rachel Bella Kahn fit all of the requirements set by the twenty-two-year-old man. She was not the first to reply to his advertisement for a bride, nor was she the applicant Abraham had initially selected. Abraham's first mail-order bride choice reconsidered the proposal after her father persuaded her that America was too far away for her to move. Rachel had no such pull in her homeland and believed her sad existence could only improve in the United States. Once she was approved by Chaya—Abraham's sister—as a suitable candidate for a wife, Rachel eagerly looked forward to beginning a new life in the fertile farmland of North Dakota.

Rachel Bella Kahn was born in 1876. Her mother died shortly after Rachel turned four, leaving her and her three siblings to be raised by their father. A servant girl was hired to help Rachel's father in tending to the children, but the girl was cruel to Rachel and her brothers and sister, denying them food and beating them. Her father remarried when Rachel was eight, but his new wife proved to be as abusive as the live-in help had been. Again the Kahn children were made to go without many of the basic necessities of life and were physically mistreated as well.

Rachel's father turned a deaf ear to his children's complaints of their stepmother's actions. The Kahn youngsters suffered through several years of cruelty. Rachel protected her family as best she could. According to her memoirs, her "childhood passed on slowly in tears."

At seventeen, Rachel went to work for her aunt as a maid. The job was a difficult one. She spent long hours cleaning the many rooms of her aunt's elaborate mansion, doing laundry, and shopping for the evening meals. Often, the shopping excursion included a trip to the butcher's shop. It was there that Rachel met and fell in love with the butcher's son. Her mother's side of the family, however, would not allow the two to pursue the relationship. They considered his occupation to be inferior and forbade them to see each other.

Rachel celebrated her eighteenth birthday alone and with no prospects for the future. She was convinced she would die an old maid. A solicitation for marriage gave her a renewed hope that she could rise above her desperate situation. Abraham Calof liked what Rachel wrote about herself in a letter of response to his search for a wife. After exchanging photos and finding favor with one another's looks, Abraham commissioned his oldest sister to further interview his prospective bride.

Chaya put Rachel through a series of strenuous tests that challenged her patience and good nature. She won the critical woman over by not becoming frustrated or angry while unraveling the ball of tangled yarn. Chaya agreed that Abraham should marry Rachel and sent her on her way.

Rachel made the journey to America traveling first by train from Brest-Litosk, Russia, to Hamburg, Germany, and then by ship to Ellis Island. She was sick for twenty of the twenty-two days at sea, but quickly forgot the discomfort the minute she saw Abraham for the first time. "There's my beloved," she told a girl sitting next to her once they arrived in New York. The engaged couple recognized each other from their photographs, and when their eyes met they knew the bond would be forever.

Rachel and Abraham traveled from Ellis Island by train to North Dakota. While en route, the pair got to know one another and Abraham revealed his plans for the future. He wanted to follow in the footsteps of his father and brothers and file a homestead claim on a patch of North Dakota prairie land. Rachel happily imagined the home she and Abraham would have, and the thought alone brought her more pleasure than she had ever known in her life.

Although Rachel instinctively knew the life of a pioneer woman would be difficult, she was not prepared for the display of hardship that greeted her upon her arrival in Devil's Lake, North Dakota. Abraham's parents, brothers, their wives, and children met the couple at the depot. Rachel was shocked by their appearance. They were dirty and dressed in rags. Their faces were weathered and none of the men wore shoes. After the introductions were made, Rachel, Abraham, and the other members of the Calof family climbed aboard an ox-led wagon and took off for their homesteads twenty-five miles from Devil's Lake.

Rachel's spirits were further dampened once they reached the Calofs' combined spread. Abraham stopped the ox team in front of one of three tiny buildings spaced a mile apart from one another. Rachel's heart sank still lower. Their home was nothing more than a rustic 12 by 14 foot, dirt-floor shack. The interior was furnished with a bed, a table made up of wood slats, two benches, and a stove. Until Rachel and Abraham exchanged vows, they would share their place with Abraham's parents, one of his brothers, his brother's wife, and their two children.

Abraham saw the disappointment in Rachel's eyes. He knew the living situation was far from perfect, but believed the sacrifice would be worth it in time. He took his fiancée on long walks, not only to get to know her better but to reassure her that these troubled times were only temporary. Rachel was encouraged by Abraham's promise that in time they would be on their own and happy.

While Abraham worked the fields, Rachel tried to make things as comfortable as she could in the primitive dwelling. Her days were spent gathering fuel for fire and greens for the evening meals, drawing water from a nearby well, and molding lamps out of dried mud. In her leisure time, she and the other members of the Calof family made plans for her and Abraham's wedding.

Rachel's memoirs are filled with tragic tales of frontier living. Her wedding day was one of the happiest times she experienced in those first few years of establishing a life on the rugged plains of North Dakota. The ceremony took place in November of 1894, and was held in the least populated Calof home. The room was decorated with wild flowers and cornhusks. All of the Calofs were in attendance as well as a pair of neighboring Jewish families. Abraham wore an ill-fitting black suit. Rachel was adorned in a wedding dress she had made herself out of yellow, blue, and white striped fabric. The music was provided by the Calof women singing traditional wedding songs, while the men kept time on tin plates.

Jewish custom dictated that Rachel's eyes be hidden throughout the day so that she could shed tears in private. During the ceremony her face was covered with a flour sack and during the reception, her eyes were covered with a cloth blindfold. After the vows were exchanged, Abraham led his bride to a banquet table filled with various dishes of beans, rice, and chicken. Once the meal was over, the couple was presented with wedding gifts—a red felt tablecloth with green flowers, two chickens, and two short women's undershirts.

Their wedding day was a festive occasion, but Rachel's joy turned to bitterness when she realized they would not be spending their wedding night alone. In order to conserve the limited fuel the combined Calof family had, they would be forced to continue sharing their home with several other people and all of the livestock. Frustrated with the living arrangements and irritated with the pungent smell from the chickens and cattle, Rachel's first day of marriage ended with her crying herself to sleep.

Abraham was determined to improve their lot. He worked long, hard hours in the field and tended to the animals. Rachel labored making bread, combing the prairie for mushrooms and other food, and milking the cows. The first winter they shared as man and wife was a cold, harsh one, but an early spring brought warmer temperatures and the glad news that they were expecting a child.

When the time came Abraham and his mother helped Rachel with the birth of the baby. They had a girl and named her Minnie. The infant was wrapped in scraps of Rachel's old shirt. The new parents were woefully lacking in material goods, but compensated for their poor conditions by showering the infant with affection.

Abraham worked nonstop in the fields to turn out a living for his wife and daughter. Rachel strived to keep her baby and herself healthy through a string of tough harvest seasons. At the end of their fifth year of marriage, the Calofs had welcomed another daughter and two sons into the world. Using the income from a successful wheat crop, Abraham built a larger home for his growing family.

By the turn of the century, it seemed as though Abraham and Rachel were on their way to transforming their once-struggling homestead into a prosperous venture. Abraham's wheat crop was the largest yet and harvest time promised to be bountiful. The Calofs would finally be able to do more than simply get by; they would see a profit from their labor.

All hope for a reversal of fortune was dashed, however, when a sudden and fierce storm dumped hail and rain over the ripe fields. It hammered the wheat into the ground and washed away the grain. Many of the Calofs' animals were killed and their home was flooded. After praising God for sparing them, they lamented their loss for a short period and then began at once to rebuild. Many neighboring settlers were unable to rebound from the disaster, but Rachel, Abraham, and their children persevered. Four years and three more children later, the Calofs' farm had fully recovered from the effects of the tragic storm.

By 1910, the Calof homestead had grown to many times the size of the original 160-acre parcel of land they initially maintained. They were not only farming but breaking and buying wild horses as well. They had earned a reputation in the territory for being tenacious and were respected for their dedication to their Jewish faith. Abraham introduced improvements in agricultural practices and marketing to new farmers on the scene, and he and Rachel helped build the first school in the area. The Calofs' efforts were recognized by Presidents William Taft and Woodrow Wilson.

The Calofs had nine children together and were married for more than fifty years. After spending twenty-three of those years on their North Dakota farm, they pulled up stakes and relocated to St. Paul, Minnesota. Abraham settled into the dry goods business and Rachel worked raising funds for a variety of charities. In 1936 she began writing her life's story.

Rachel and Abraham both died from natural causes in their late seventies. Rachel called their marital and pioneer experience "a life worth living."

ELINORE PRUITT & CLYDE STEWART
The Homesteader and the Sheep Rancher

The thing I have done is to marry Mr. Stewart. It was such an inconsistent thing to do that I was ashamed to tell you. And, too, I was afraid you would think I didn't need your friendship and might desert me.

Elinore Pruitt Stewart's letter to friend
and former employee Mrs. Coney—July 16, 1910

*E*linore Pruitt's thick, gloved hands unfolded a newspaper advertisement and followed the words written across the page with her index finger. "Housekeeper-cook wanted for respected land owner. Offering a good permanent home for the right party." The announcement, placed in a Colorado newspaper in April 1909, was submitted by Wyoming sheep rancher H. Clyde Stewart. Elinore's soft eyes studied the name of the rancher for a moment. She said his name out loud a few times and decided it was a good strong name. A dependable name, she told herself as she refolded the advertisement and slid it into her pocket.

She smoothed out the slight wrinkles in her blue gingham dress and shifted in her seat. She glanced nervously at the mantle clock in Boulder's Sunshine Mission, where she and her two-year-old daughter, Jerrine, lived. Clyde would soon be there to interview her. If all went well, she would be on her way to Wyoming within the week.

Since the death of her husband Amelie Rupert in 1905, Elinore had dreamed of going west and becoming a homesteader. Responding to Clyde's proposition was her way of taking control of her destiny.

Clyde Stewart entered the mission at the exact time they were scheduled to meet. He was a proud, confident man of Scottish descent who Elinore later bragged "stood inspection admirably." They were quite impressed with one another. Elinore thought his demeanor and accent were quite charming. Clyde, ten years Elinore's senior, found her to be a "lovely lass with a delightful sense of humor." After a brief question-and-answer period, Elinore was invited to join Clyde on his trip to Burnt Fork, Wyoming.

Elinore Pruitt's life had begun in Fort Smith, Arkansas, in 1876. The oldest in a family of nine, she assumed responsibility for her siblings after her parents died. At fourteen, she was a high school student, caretaker of her brothers, and a part-time employee with the Transcontinental Railroad. She was very well read and enjoyed writing. At the age of twenty-two, she married a man who gave her the chance to capitalize on her talent. He encouraged her writing and persuaded her to regularly contribute articles and short stories to the *Kansas City Star.* Four years after she married the inspiring Amelie Rupert, and only a few months after the birth of their daughter, he was killed in a train accident.

With the notion of some day owning her own plot of land, Elinore drifted west, taking jobs along the way as a cook and laundress. In Denver, Colorado, Elinore befriended Ida Coney and for a time worked preparing the aristocratic woman's meals and tending to her home. Although she and her young daughter were fond of Mrs. Coney, Elinore was not content to stay in Denver. While in town one day loading up on supplies, she overheard two men discussing land in Wyoming available for homesteading. The conversation gave her incentive to continue pursuing her life's ambition, and in February of 1909, she wrote in her journal, "Nothing but the mountains, the pines, and the clean, fresh air seemed worthwhile . . . I want a homestead. One under my own name."

Elinore began at once making plans to fulfill her dream. The pastor of her church discouraged her from making the journey to Wyoming alone. He persuaded her to answer Clyde's ad, arguing the need to align herself with someone who already knew the territory and could give her sound advice. It was a sensible request and she complied.

Elinore, Jerrine, and Clyde arrived in Wyoming in April of 1909. It took three days traveling by train and stage to reach their destination. The stage ride over rough terrain was uncomfortable, and the road leading into Burnt Fork was covered in melting snow and mud. As soon as Elinore and her daughter were settled in at the Stewart ranch, she sat down to write Mrs. Coney to assure her of their safety.

At last we arrived, and everything is just lovely for me. I have a very, very comfortable situation and Mr. Stewart is absolutely no trouble, for as soon as he has his meals he retires to his room and plays on his bagpipes—only he calls it his 'bugpeep.' There is a saddle horse especially for me and a little shotgun with which I am to kill sage chickens. We are between two trout streams, so you can think of me as being happy when the snow is through melting and the water gets clear . . . Jerrine is making good use of all the good things we are having. She rides the pony to water every day.

I have not filed on my land yet because the snow is fifteen feet deep on it, and I think I would rather see what I am getting, so will wait until summer. They have just three seasons here, winter and July and August. We are to plant our garden the last of May. When it is so I can get around I will see about land and find out all I can and tell you.

Elinore Pruitt Rupert—April 18, 1909

In May 1909, Elinore laid claim to a homestead, filing on land adjoining Clyde's. The two worked their plots, mowing and stacking hay, planting gardens, and tending to the livestock. When she wasn't busy managing the farm and cooking, Elinore and Jerrine would saddle a pony and ride across the hills surrounding the property. Mother and daughter followed renegade streams into the mountains, chased clouds in the big sky, and basked in the glorious colors and beautiful sunsets. Elinore had never known such happiness.

Any woman who can stand her own company, can see the beauty of the sunset, loves growing things, and is willing to put in as much time at careful labor as she does over the washtub, will certainly succeed; will have independence, plenty to eat all the time, and a home of her own in the end.

Elinore Pruitt Rupert—January 23, 1913

Within six weeks of her stay at Clyde's, the two had fallen in love and married. She did not regret the short engagement or the hasty wedding. The demands of caring for the ranch necessitated the quick nuptials. As she wrote in a 1912 letter to Ida Coney, "Between planting the oats and other work that must be done early . . .Wyoming ranchers can scarcely take time even to be married in the springtime." In that same letter, written two years after the couple had married, Elinore shared the events leading up to her wedding.

I have often wished I might tell you all about my Clyde, but have not because of two things. One is I could not even begin without telling you what a good man he is, and I didn't want you to think I could do nothing but brag. The other reason is the haste I married in . . . The license was sent for by mail, and as soon as it came Mr. Stewart saddled Chub and went down to the house of Mr. Pearson, the justice of the peace and a friend of long standing. I had never met any of the family and naturally rather dreaded to have them come, but Mr. Stewart was firm in wanting to be married at home, so he told Mr. Pearson he wanted him and his family to come up the following Wednesday and serve papers on the "wooman i' the hoose." They were astonished, of course, but being such good friends they promised him all the assistance they could render. They are quite the dearest, most interesting family! I have since learned to love them as my own.

Well there was no time to make wedding clothes, so I had to "do up" what I did have. Isn't it queer how sometimes, do what you can, work will keep getting in the way until you can't get anything done? That is how it was with me those few days before the wedding; so much so that when Wednesday dawned everything was topsy-turvy and I had a very strong desire to run away. But I always did hate a "piker," so I stood pat. Well, I had most of the dinner cooked, but it kept me hustling to get the house into anything like decent order before

68

the old dog barked, and I knew my moments of liberty were limited. It was blowing a perfect hurricane and snowing like midwinter. I had bought a beautiful pair of shoes to wear on that day, but my vanity had squeezed my feet a little, so while I was so busy at work I had kept on a worn old pair, intending to put on the new ones later; but when the Pearsons drove up all I thought about was getting them into the house where there was fire, so I forgot all about the old shoes and the apron I wore.

I had only been here six weeks then, and was a stranger. That is why I had no one to help me and was so confused and hurried. As soon as the newcomers were warm, Mr. Stewart told me I had better come over by him and stand up. It was a large room I had to cross, and how I did it before all those strange eyes I never knew. All I can remember very distinctly is hearing Mr. Stewart saying, "I will," and myself chiming in that I would, too. Happening to glance down, I saw that I had forgotten to take off my apron or my old shoes, but just then Mr. Pearson pronounced us man and wife, and as I had dinner to serve right away I had no time to worry over my odd toilet.

Elinore Pruitt Stewart—December 2, 1912

According to Elinore's letters to Ida, the Stewarts lived a quiet, but idyllic life in their home among the blue mountains. Elinore wrote her friend that when she thought of all she had to be thankful for, she could scarcely crowd her joy into one short life.

The Stewarts knew tragedy as well as joy, however, and Elinore held the family together through those difficult times with unwavering courage. Clyde and Elinore's first son was born a year after they were married but died of *erysipelas* (an acute disease of the skin) a few months later. Elinore's letter to Ida reflected the grace with which she accepted the hardship.

I held him in my arms till the last agony was over. Then I dressed the beautiful little body for the grave. Clyde is a carpenter; so I wanted him to make the little coffin. He did it every bit, and I lined and padded it, trimmed and covered it. Not that we couldn't afford to buy one or that our neighbors were not all that was kind and willing; but because it was a sad pleasure to do everything for our little first-born ourselves.

As there had been no physician to help, so there was no minister to comfort, and I could not bear to let our baby leave the world without leaving any message to a community that sadly needed it. His little message to us had been love, so I selected a chapter from John and we had a funeral service, at which all our neighbors for thirty miles around were present. So you see, our union is sealed by love and welded by a great sorrow.

Elinore Pruitt Stewart—December 2, 1912

Elinore gave Clyde three more sons and all grew to be fine men. The Stewarts were married for twenty-four years. Throughout the first four years of their marriage, Elinore corresponded with Ida Coney, sharing with her the adventures of a woman homesteader. In 1913 those letters were bound in a published book, *Letters of a Woman Homesteader.*

In 1926, Elinore suffered a serious injury while she was out stacking hay. A covey of quail flew in front of the horse-drawn mower she was driving. The horses spooked and bolted, in the process tossing her in front of the machine. She never fully recovered from the accident and subsequently died in 1933. She was fifty-seven years old.

TROUBLE ON A BRIDAL TOUR

*I*n 1886, passengers aboard the Union Pacific Railroad, traveling from Riverside across California, were aghast at an overt display of affection between a groom and his mail-order bride. The blissful couple, excited about their marriage, fawned over each other so much that their fellow riders complained. The following is an article about the so-called "appalling event:"

Now, what's the use of it? When a couple get married and go off on a bridal tour, why so misbehave themselves as to be "spotted" by every man, woman and child on the train for "fresh fish?" How silly the thing must appear to them when they look back after a period of six months. Are we fools when in love, and are we idiots when we marry?

The couple I have in mind had a seat in the middle of the car. She was his'n and he was her'n. All the tomfoolery of courtship days was over. The preacher had made things right, and her father would no longer set the dog on him or place torpedoes around the gate. She didn't show the least disposition to jump out of the car window, but all the sudden, he grabbed her by the paw. She grabbed back. Then he leaned over at an angle of 45 degrees, and she fell toward him.

It was a very uncomfortable position, but they maintained it with scarcely any change for hours. Her hat got skewed around almost hind side before, but she would not release her clutch for fear he'd go through the roof. His collar wilted and his necktie worked around under his ear, but if he let go of her paw she'd think he was mad.

"Darling!" said he in a bullfrog whisper, "doesn't it seem funny?"

"I can't realize it," she answered as she raked one of her back hairpins across his nose.

Commandments of California Wives. Entered according to act of Congress in the year 1855 in the Clerk's office on the U.S. District Court of California.

"All mine?"

"Yes, lovely."

"Never get mad?"

"Never, sweety."

The man on the seat behind them folded up the paper, picked up his grip, and changed to a seat across the aisle. As he sat down a motherly looking woman inquired:

"Are they married?"

"I think so, madam. A mail-order match I overheard."

"And can nothing be done to stop it?"

"I think not."

For two or three minutes, the newly wedded were silent.

"Darling!" she sighed.

"What is it? If any base hyena has dared to cause you a moment's unhappiness, I'll murder him! Point out the animal."

"It isn't that."

"Then what?"

"I'm—afraid you'll be mad."

"No, I won't. How could I be mad at you? What is it, Dolly?"

"Why, I wish you'd wipe the sweat out of that left ear. Now, you love me just the same, don't you?"

"Of course."

"And you aren't mad?"

"Why, no. There, now—who cares who's looking. It's nobody's business anyhow."

There was another interval of silence during which she tried to remember whether they were engaged the week before her father gave Henry the book, or whether it was the next Sunday after.

"Henwy?"

"What angel?"

"Are we weally married?"

"Yes, love."

"And you love me?"

"With all my heart."

"And you aren't mad?"

"No, dearest."

"Then I'm so happy! Henry squeeze my hand."

He squose. We held an indignation meeting and appointed a committee to see if something could not be done, but he squose the harder.

Three or four women got together and passed a resolution to the effect that if a railroad company could not protect its passengers the legislature should be appealed to, but that couple had a death grip on each other and wouldn't let go.

The baggage man came in when sent for, but he said he was helpless. He knew just how we must feel but the railroad wasn't to blame. The conductor came back to the car and asked us not to lay it up against him. He was a poor man, had been out of a job several months, and this was his first run.

Well, the long and short of the matter was that eighteen or twenty of us rode 150 miles wishing we had not gotten on the train, and resolving that the thing will never happen again—never. We shook hands on that and agreed that we'd walk first.

The *Daily Press*, Riverside, California—July 10, 1886

THE RED STOCKING SNOOZERS

A cold Sierra wind blew past the lace-curtained window of a quaint Victorian home overlooking the lush Nevada City, California, terrain. Inside, three elegantly dressed ladies sat fireside, sipping tea and discussing the rough elements who lived and worked in the town's mining camps. It was 1878, and the hills across the Gold Country were filled with unattached, rambunctious prospectors. Once the sun had set and they could no longer work their claims, they made their way to the saloons to drink away their free time. Refined females considered such behavior to be an abomination and the source of great trouble. The proper ladies at the tea party believed the love of a good woman could deter coarse miners from these depraved activities and bring about civility in their community.

Taking a cue from other frontier entrepreneurs, the women decided to make a written appeal to single females in the East to come to the West. With the abundance of available men in the region, the ladies were hopeful numerous matches would be made. Several obstacles needed to be overcome, however, before such a venture could be launched.

Lack of funding to support such a grand endeavor would be a major hurdle, but first there was a local group that needed to be dealt with before any potential brides arrived. Young bachelors in the area had organized a secret society whose principal object was the suppression of the female sex.

Members of the newly organized "Tea Trio" society recognized the necessity of disbanding the bachelor society, and plans were made to bring about its demise. They sought a young reporter with a local newspaper, and, promising the timid man a bride of his own, asked him to join the bachelors' secret club and publish his findings. In case he should meet with an untimely death, the ladies promised to defray the expense of his funeral.

The eager young man set to work and made inquiries of those suspected of being members of the group. After tackling half a dozen, one society bachelor willing to share information with the reporter was found. The gentleman wasn't an inducted part of the organization yet, but he had a friend who was. The friend agreed to submit the reporter's name to the group, and if he was accepted, his initiation would follow that night.

The following article, written by the journalist about his experience, appeared in the Nevada County newspaper, the *Daily Transcript.*

My application was favorably received at the next regular meeting. I had gone to bed. It was 11:30 p.m. when I was informed by the committee of my success, and led to the place of the meeting in the bushes half way up the north side of Sugar Loaf. I was blindfolded and the initiation ceremony was most peculiar. Finally, the bandage (a lady's lace handkerchief) was removed in response to an order like this, "Proclaim the fact of his redemption and let the blind behold!"

The sight that met this reporter's eyes cannot be adequately described. The members sat in a circle on the ground. In the absence of President Mike Garver, Jerry Payne was called to the chair, or rather a boulder, which answered the same purpose. Joe Fleming and George Stewart were hanging on to a monstrous banner to keep it from being blown over by the breeze. On this banner was inscribed the name of the order "THE RED STOCKING SNOOZERS." Am Lord, Dex Ridley and L. Sukeforth were taking turns throwing wood upon the campfire that illumined the mysterious scene, and at the same time discussing topics of current interest, such as the new style of fall bonnets, etc.

The two Fulweiler Brothers were playing seven-up with the queens left out of the pack. M. Rosenburg and H. Hirshman had been stationed one on the summit and the other at the foot of Sugar Loaf to give warning of approaching danger.

Among other names proposed for membership during the evening were those of Walter Vinton, Fred Searls and Archie Nivens. George Hentz moved that the applications be allowed to remain over for one month. Hentz seconded his own motion. It was put to a vote and carried unanimously. Everything was going along smoothly until Am Lord discovered the President pro-tem wearing a white vest and mauve-colored necktie. This created a suspicion among the members that Jerry's faith was weakening. He saw the storm brewing, and

French advertisement, 1857. A French woman stands between two mines where California Argonauts bid for her affections and the chance to be her husband.

rising, began to speak. In a few well chosen words, he sharply criticized former members who had "for years" shared the benefits of the society, and had basely deserted it, "seeming" he added, "to embrace the first opportunity. A woman!"

"I call the gentlemen to order," hastily interrupted John Bacigalupi. "If the President knows anything he knows that according to the Constitution the name of wo____, that is to say fe____, of course you understand, the other sex of our species is not to be spoken of or about on such occasion as this."

The president glared upon the crowd and singling out Si Jackson who lately joined and was extremely bashful, fastened his eye upon him and said sternly, "Sit down!"

"Go to thunder!" was the prompt response.

Charley Fulweiler smiled approvingly, but detecting the president looking at him with considerable austerity, squirmed so that he put his foot in the hat of Jesse Holcomb, who had dropped in, in a friendly sort of way.

"Now gentlemen, what I want to say is this," said H. Hirshman, who had left his post at the foot of the hill to join the conclave. "We need a higher discipline in our organization. We need so to speak, a sort of spartan firmness, we need . . ."

"You will need to get your lives insured before we get through with you," shrieked a female voice a short distance away. "Gim'me the club, Sarah. Oh, gimme it quick!"

There was the sound of rushing skirts through the bushes. The meeting adjourned in confusion, and the members scattered in every direction.

The guards had been negligent in their duties, and when the indignant Tea Trio reached the scene of the "Red Stocking" deliberations, there wasn't a young man to be found.

Harris Longfield—March 3, 1878

There is no historical information available to indicate that the Red Stocking Snoozers continued to get together after their encounter with the Tea Trio. The Trio did continue to meet but shifted their focus from matchmaking to raising funds for orphans.

ELIZA FARNHAM
The Dedicated Sponsor

The mission is a good one, and the projector deserves success.
The enterprise in which Mrs. Farnham has engaged is one
which evinces much moral courage. Her reward will be
found in the blessings, which her countrymen will invoke for
her when the vessel in which the association is to sail shall
have arrived in California with her precious cargo. May
favoring gales attend the good ship Angelique.

Horace Greeley, Newspaperman
—April 12, 1849

Eliza Farnham stepped off the spacious packet ship *Angelique,* docked in the San Francisco harbor, and scanned the bustling, seaside city with a smile. The pier was lined with curious, enthusiastic men waiting to introduce themselves to the more than 200 young ladies who had replied to Eliza's ad seeking marriageable women to accompany her to the West. Taking the hand of each of her young sons, she proceeded proudly down the gangplank. All eyes were fixed on the thin, bespectacled author and lecturer, on her intelligent, deep-set eyes, and her dark hair arranged in prim ringlets around her face. She stopped and waited for her charges to disembark. Just three ladies who dared to take the trip across the ocean followed after Eliza.

The happy expressions the hopeful men wore were at once replaced with disappointed sneers. Lonely miners, who had come to California seeking a fortune in gold in 1849, were eagerly looking forward to seeing members of the opposite sex. Men outnumbered women on the emerging frontier by more than twelve to one. When news of Eliza's trip to the Gold Country reached their desperate ears, they believed she would be bringing 10,000 eligible ladies with her.

Disgruntled pioneers from every profession took to the saloons to drink away their dreams of finding a wife among Eliza's few recruits. The streets were soon filled with intoxicated men using their fists to work out their frustrations. Miner Dashel Greech reported of the scene: "I verily believe there was more drunkenness, more gambling, more fighting, and more of everything that was bad that night, than ever before occurred in San Francisco within any similar space of time."

It was precisely this volatile, dissolute way of life that Eliza sought to correct. She believed the gentling influence of good women could bring positive lasting changes for western pioneers and miners, and could help tame the Wild West in the process. Many notable historians described her at the time as "a woman bent on doing the world as much good as possible."

Born on November 17, 1815, in Rensselaerville, New York, Eliza Woodson Burhans was raised by an overbearing aunt and drunkard uncle. Her mother passed away when she was five, and she never knew her father. Her upbringing was strict and troubled, plagued with abuse and neglect. She managed to rise above her struggles, however, finding solace in her schoolwork, as well as in books by Voltaire and Thomas Paine.

In 1835, at the age of twenty, Eliza made her first trip west, traveling over the Santa Cruz mountains in a buggy. The trip was grueling, but exhilarating for the young woman who gained strength in the beauty of the open country. She had read about the spacious landscape of the western frontier and wanted to see the unsettled prairie firsthand. She considered the new territory "a wholly honest place where mankind could push the boundaries of all he believed possible in himself and his world."

Upon her return from her adventures out West, she moved to Illinois to live with her sister and brother-in-law. It was there, in the Prairie State, that she met a young New England lawyer named Thomas Jefferson Farnham. After a brief courtship the pair married in the fall of 1836. Eliza, who never saw herself as attractive, was transformed by Thomas's love. "I never imagined myself clothed with external splendor, or gifted with beauty,

Eliza Farnham

until approving eyes gazed upon me," she wrote.

Thomas moved his new bride into a quaint two-room cottage, and presented her with a chestnut pony as a wedding gift. For a while they were blissfully happy.

In 1838, she gave birth to their first son. But the following year the couple watched him suffer with yellow fever and die. The disease also took her sister's life. She buried the pair together. "It is a devastating time," she wrote, "My sister is gone and my boy. His little coffin . . . seemed to carry my very heart into the earth with it."

Thomas mourned the loss by taking a job as leader of an emigrant party heading to Oregon. Eliza remained behind, pouring her sorrows out on paper. She traveled throughout Illinois by stagecoach, compiling notes for a book she hoped to one day write.

Not long after Thomas returned from his overland trek, he moved his wife east to New York. He wrote extensively about his trip across the frontier, and by 1846 had published four guidebooks. After giving Thomas two more sons, Eliza realized her dream of seeing her own work in print. Her first manuscript, published in 1843, focused on what she called "a woman's moral and spiritual superiority." Her subsequent work centered on the same theme, pondering the importance of a woman's role as a civilizer in frontier society. Her profound declarations and ideas shocked most readers, generated attention from politicians, and prompted a job offer from the Sing Sing Prison, where she was invited to serve as jail matron for the women's section.

Eliza was twenty-seven when she accepted the position at Sing Sing, and she set about immediately to change the cruel ways in which female inmates were treated. She brought the establishment out of its dark age, where harsh fire-and-brimstone religiosity was practiced, and into a new era where prisoners were supplied with books and taught to read.

Feeling restless and increasingly resentful of Eliza's popularity as a reformer, Thomas went west again in 1847. A year later, while visiting San Francisco, he fell ill and died from complications of pneumonia. Once Eliza heard of Thomas's death, she left at once for California. With her arms around her sons, nine-year-old Charles and eleven-year-old Edward, Eliza walked through the muddy, unpaved San Francisco streets toward the mortuary. Rowdy men filled every thoroughfare, parading from gaudy gambling house to gaudy saloon and back again like ants. Bawdy music spilled out of windows and doors of the bars, and guns fired at all hours of the night. Eliza drank in what she deemed "a wild, depraved scene—the reckless abandon of a city raging with Gold Rush fever."

The lack of women in this rambunctious setting did not escape her attention. She was one of a handful of females in the Gold Country and wherever she went, men stared at her. "Doorways filled instantly," she wrote, "little islands in the street were thronged with men who seemed to gather in a moment, and who remained immovable until I passed."

Recalling her belief that women were "civilizers in a frontier society," a plan began to take shape. "If this rugged area were to be reformed—it would take women to bring that change about," she later wrote. After a short rest, Eliza began the journey back to the East Coast with the idea to petition single women to move to California as "checks upon the many evils" there.

On February 2, 1849, Eliza drafted an advertisement to be published in New York papers that explained her intentions:

> It is proposed that the company shall consist of persons not under twenty-five years of age, who shall bring from their clergyman, or some authority of the town where they reside, satisfactory testimonials of education, character, capacity, etc., and who can contribute the sum of two hundred and fifty dollars, to defray the expenses of the voyage, make suitable provision for their accommodation after reaching San Francisco, until they shall be able to enter upon some occupation for their support, and create a fund to be held in reserve for the relief of any who may be ill, or otherwise need aid before they are able to provide for themselves.

To give her advertisement an air of respectability and authority she hoped would further attract prospective brides, she secured endorsements

SHIP ANGELIQUE.

CALIFORNIA ASSOCIATION OF AMERICAN WOMEN.

NEW YORK. FEBRUARY 2D, 1849.

THE death of my husband, THOMAS J. FARNHAM, Esq., at San Francisco, in September last. renders it expedient that I should visit California during the coming season. Having a desire to accomplish some greater good by my journey thither than to give the necessary attention to my private affairs, and believing that the presence of women would be one of the surest checks upon many of the evils that are apprehended there, I desire to ask attention to the following sketch of a plan for organizing a party of such persons to emigrate to that country.

Among the many privations and deteriorating influences to which the thousands who are flocking thither will be subjected, one of the greatest is the absence of woman, with all her kindly cares and powers, so peculiarly conservative to man under such circumstances.

It would exceed the limits of this circular to hint at the benefits that would flow to the growing population of that wonderful region, from the introduction among them of intelligent, virtuous and efficient women. Of such only. it is proposed to make up this company. It is believed that there are hundreds, if not thousands, of such females in our country who are not bound by any tie that would hold them here, who might, by going thither, have the satisfaction of employing themselves greatly to the benefit and advantage of those who are there, and at the same time of serving their own interest more effectually than by following any employment that offers to them here.

It is proposed that the company shall consist of persons not under twenty-five years of age. who shall bring from their clergyman, or some authority of the town where they reside, satisfactory testimonials of education. character. capacity. &c., and who can contribute the sum of two hundred and fifty dollars, to defray the expenses of the voyage. make suitable provision for their accommodation after reaching San Francisco, until they shall be able to enter upon some occupation for their support. and create a fund to be held in reserve for the relief of any who may be ill. or otherwise need aid before they are able to provide for themselves.

It is believed that such an arrangement, with one hundred or one hundred and thirty persons. would enable the company to purchase or charter a vessel, and fit it up with every thing necessary to comfort on the voyage. and that the combination of all for the support of each, would give such security, both as to health. person and character, as would remove all reasonable hesitation from the minds of those who may be disposed and able to join such a mission. It is intended that the party shall include six or eight respectable married men and their families.

Those who desire further information will receive it by calling on the subscriber at

ELIZA W FARNHAM.

The New-York built Packet Ship ANGELIQUE has been engaged to take out this Association. She is a spacious vessel. fitted up with state rooms throughout and berths of good size, well ventilated and provided in every way to secure a safe. speedy and comfortable voyage. She will be ready to sail from New-York about the 12th or 15th of April

WE, the undersigned, having been made acquainted with the plan proposed by MRS. FARNHAM, in the above circular, hereby express our approbation of the same, and recommend her to those who may be disposed to unite with her in it. as worthy the trust and confidence necessary to its successful conduct.

HON. J. W. EDMONDS, Judge Superior Court
HON. W. T. McCOUN, Late Vice Chancellor.
HON. B. F. BUTLER, Late U. S. Attorney.
HON. H. GREELEY.
ISAAC T. HOPPER, ESQ.
FREEMAN HUNT, ESQ.
THOMAS C. DOREMUS, ESQ.

W. C. BRYANT, ESQ.
SHEPHERD KNAPP, ESQ.
REV. GEORGE POTTS. D. D.
REV. HENRY WARD BEECHER.
Miss CATHARINE M. SEDGWICK.
MRS. C. M. KIRKLAND

NESBITT. PRINTER.

Reformer Eliza Farnham authored this broadside encouraging single women to come West and act as "cheers upon many of the evils there."

from leading political figures like Horace Greeley, William Cullen Bryant, and Henry Ward Beecher. More than 200 ladies responded to Eliza's broadside, but a sudden illness kept her from being able to actively organize the expedition. In the end, only a handful of brides-to-be agreed to go to California with her.

Eliza and her entourage set sail on April 15, 1849. The trip was widely publicized in frontier newspapers. Lonely miners eagerly anticipated the arrival of the packet ship *Angelique*, hoping to find a wife among its gentle freight. Some men, such as miner Henry Holmes, made mention of the forthcoming event in their daily journals. "Went to church three times today," Holmes reported, "A few ladies present, does my eye good to see a woman once more. Hope Mrs. Farnham will bring 10,000."

Not everyone found the idea of supplying single pioneers with potential brides acceptable. Many socialites considered it a scandalous plan, and the campaign was mired in controversy. Rumors that Eliza was little more than a procurer ultimately kept many women from committing to the journey.

The highly anticipated trip to San Francisco was troublesome from the start. Eliza challenged the authority of the ship's captain, demanding he make an unscheduled stop for fresh water. Furious with what he referred to as a "brazen female meddler," the captain lured Eliza and her charges off the ship in Chile and left them stranded there. A long, anxious month passed before they were able to catch another ship for San Francisco. Eliza and her boys arrived at their new home in Santa Cruz in February of 1850, and from there proceeded to find the land that had been left to them. After a short carriage ride through the country, the three arrived at the homestead. The house itself was little more than a shack, but the acreage around it was lush and filled with cattle. "An ideal place to raise a family," she would later write in her book, *California, In-Doors and Out.*

With the help of her good friend, Georgiana Bruce Kirby, the two built a ranch house on the property and began farming the land. Realizing their long, full dresses hampered their work in the fields, Eliza decided the two needed to wear bloomers. She made their wide, loose pants from old gymnastic suits. Like her mail-order bride plan, it was another unconventional action that shocked the community around her.

In 1852, Eliza accepted a marriage proposal from San Francisco resident and entrepreneur, William Alexander Fitzpatrick. According to

Georgiana's journal, William was the "greatest blackguard in the country." He frequently mistreated Eliza and their life was a series of stormy partings and reconciliations. The two divorced four years later.

In 1856, Eliza abandoned ranch life and returned to her work at state women's prisons, speaking out for reform. She eventually took a job as principal of the first Santa Cruz public school. In her leisure time she toured the state, lecturing on topics ranging from spiritualism to women's rights. She penned four books on the subject of women and the emerging West. In 1859, she organized a society to assist destitute women in finding homes in the West, and took charge of several such emigrant parties. "None but the pure and strong-hearted of my sex should come alone to this land," she reasoned.

Historian Herbert Bancroft boasted that Eliza was one of the "first women to recognize the effects her sex could have on the Wild West—and probably one to be avoided at all costs by the hell-raising male population in the California gold fields." Her efforts convinced like-minded female pioneers to relocate and cast their influence over the new frontier.

This is the most gladdening intelligence of the day . . . Eliza Farnham and her girls are coming, and the dawning of brighter days for our golden land is even now perceptible. The day of regeneration is nigh on hand . . . We shall . . . prepare ourselves to witness the great change which is shortly to follow, with feelings akin to hilarious joy.

California Daily Alta—1849

Eliza Farnham's unconventional methods of bringing civility to the Wild West helped transform the frontier and make the emerging country fit for wives and family.

BRIDAL COUPLES

*D*uring the late 1880s, Gold Country hostelries were literally filled with blushing brides. Women arrived from eastern locations to wed the men they'd met through mail-order advertisements and set up house in the rich hills of northern California. San Francisco was one of the most popular places in the country to honeymoon. Couples found it to be a cheerful city with enough sights to occupy their time for months. The presence of many new partners gave the location a sense of solace that helped make the mail-order pairs feel at home as well. San Francisco innkeepers competed for the business of honeymooning couples, offering them a variety of goods and services in return for staying at their establishments. The rivalry between the hotels was fierce and often made front-page news.

So great has become the competition between three or four of the leading city's hotels in the solicitation for bridal couples that the most successful of the landlords in this effort presents each one of the brides who stop at his hostelry a beautiful bouquet or basket of cut flowers. The clerk who receives the couple inquires of the bridegroom if he suspects a recent marriage—and it is seldom that a mistake is made—and then the flowers go up to the apartments engaged.

One of the most lucrative classes for the landlords is the newly married. Beginning in October and ending in April, it is estimated that there are in the city an average all the time of two hundred pairs of brides and grooms. The manager of the hotel which entertains most of them says he frequently has forty couples, and averages over twenty-five during the busy season. They are, he says, the most desirable class of guests. Always pleasant, they want the best of everything, and are given it. This hostelry makes a feature of pleasing those people,

M. Willisume exportant en Californie un *article* qui est excessivement demandé.

French advertisement, 1857. A marriage broker packages brides set for shipment to California, where women are in high demand.

and all embarrassments are lessened to the minimum. Guests there are so used to seeing large numbers of brides and grooms that they are spared the stares so customary where this class is rare.

It is said to be the purpose of the great hotel company organizing here, and which intends to build a structure at a cost of $2,500,000, to arrange one floor with bridal apartments.

Matrimonial News—January 1887

KATHLEEN FORRESTSTALL
Irish Bride in Waiting

A weather-beaten stage labored over a rocky incline, then came to a stop to give the tired team of horses a chance to rest. Three road-weary passengers emerged from the coach and looked around. Eighteen-year-old Kathleen Forreststall was among them. She was a tall woman with red hair, green eyes, and a shocking number of freckles scattered across her face. She stared down at the valley below and at Fort Klamath in the near distance. She had left her home in County Cork, Ireland, on March 10, 1853. Five months later she was now looking out over the Oregon territory that was to be her new home.

Kathleen's journey to the West had been a difficult one. Since reaching the states, she'd encountered rugged terrain, torrential downpours, and hostile Indians, and been robbed of her life savings. Nevertheless, considering the tragic life she had left behind in her homeland, these struggles were much more bearable.

Kathleen was born on November 16, 1835, in Waterford, Ireland. Her parents were farmers who had seven children to help them work a thirty-two acre plot of land that belonged to a British couple. She was the oldest girl and dreamed of becoming a schoolteacher. Kathleen was an exceptional student, and her mother and father encouraged her in all of her scholastic endeavors. When she was fourteen, however, a countrywide famine forced her to reevaluate her life's pursuit.

By the time Kathleen became a teenager, the population in Ireland was more than eight million. There were few industries, so the country depended largely on agriculture. Farms decreased in size as the population grew. Most of the people, such as the Forreststalls, lived as tenants on the small farms they worked, and most of the produce they raised had to be turned over to the landlord as rent. Kathleen's family, and others like them, had to struggle to survive on what was left from their production.

In 1848, a blight or disease infected the crops, rotting potatoes. Millions faced starvation. During the time of the first failed crops, Kathleen lost her mother and five of her siblings to hunger and sickness. Many of Kathleen's neighbors and friends were emigrating out of the country and making their way to America or Canada. Kathleen, having watched her family starve, determined she would leave Ireland as soon as she could raise the money to do so.

An opportunity arose when a doctor who was paying a visit to the Forreststall home shared a copy of a San Francisco paper with Kathleen. The publication contained ads from pioneers and western settlers searching for wives, and many articles told of the shortage of women in the remote areas of the West and the opportunities available for adventurous females seeking a new life. Kathleen poured over the advertisements looking for a suitable solicitor. Within the numerous announcements was a plea from a young soldier: "In the interest of lifelong companionship and devotion—I am submitting this notice. I am a soldier with the United States Army. I am 27 years of age and of good, sturdy stock. I would like to correspond with a lady interested in matrimony."

Lieutenant Fred M. Carey—1851

Kathleen sent a letter off to Lieutenant Carey describing her background, religious views, physical appearance, and desire to marry. Their written courtship was short, and the lieutenant proposed to Kathleen in his second letter. He also sent along the funds necessary for her to make her way to America.

After bidding farewell to her father and sisters, she boarded a ship and set sail in search of a better life. The voyage across the Atlantic was challenging.

Kathleen was hundreds of miles from Ireland but still feeling the pangs of hunger, because the vessel was poorly equipped with provisions. She survived on stale crackers and tea until the ship docked at the Isthmus of Panama, where she was able to purchase bananas and bread. She befriended another woman on the journey and the two spent a great deal of time together, swapping secrets and plans for the future. Kathleen foolishly told her new confidant the hiding place for the money sent to her by the lieutenant. Before the ship made port again, the woman had stolen $300 that Kathleen had sewn into the lining of one of her dresses.

When Kathleen arrived in San Francisco, she was virtually penniless. She sent a wire to the groom-to-be, and Lieutenant Carey arranged to pay for her stage fare. After a long, grueling ride, the coach arrived at Fort Klamath. Kathleen's lieutenant was there to meet her.

Fred Carey was a shy, unassuming, slightly balding man who stood barely over five-feet-five-inches tall. The two smiled at one another and politely shook hands. He escorted her to the Fort's guest quarters and after giving her a chance to unpack, the two set out for a walk.

Kathleen and Fred spent two days getting to know each other. He explained the vagabond lifestyle of a soldier and she agreed to take on all the responsibilities that were expected of an Army wife. A wedding date was set for the next time a minister would be at the Fort. A pair of officers' wives offered to help Kathleen make preparations for the big day.

A week before Fred and Kathleen exchanged vows, the lieutenant was ordered to escort a supply wagon to Fort Walla Walla in the northern portion of the state. The couple said their goodbyes and the lieutenant promised to hurry back. As he left, Kathleen realized for the first time how much she had become attached to him. She had not anticipated falling in love but, happily, she had.

During Fred's absence, a social was held in honor of the Fort's commanding officer's birthday. An array of food was served, parlor games were played, and there was music and dancing. Kathleen joined in the festivities, contributing a pie to the banquet and agreeing to dance with some of the soldiers. She had a delightful time and made sure those around her were equally as joyful.

Upon Fred's return, the men in his service complimented him on his choice for a wife. They bragged about her cooking and talent as a dancer. Fred was horrified to learn that his intended had engaged in such "inappropriate" behavior while he was away. He confronted Kathleen, who, seeing no harm in what she had done, confessed to the actions.

The outraged and humiliated lieutenant called off the wedding. Kathleen begged him to reconsider, but he refused. Adding insult to injury, he demanded the money he invested in his mail-order bride be returned.

In order to earn the funds needed to repay Fred, Kathleen took on the job as the Fort's laundry woman. Once financial restitution had been made, she relocated to San Francisco. Historical records show that she answered another advertisement for a mail-order bride, and this time, successfully married the ad's author. The newlyweds moved to a mining camp in Placer County and opened a boarding house.

Lieutenant Fred M. Carey never married.

THE NEW PLAN
Magazine for Matrimony

*T*ears slid down widow Mabel Haskell's face and fell onto the blank piece of paper in front of her. She sat poised, pen in hand over the monogrammed stationery, contemplating her life and lamenting her cheerless state of affairs. The sad but striking-looking woman in her late forties had no family, no children of her own, and had lost her husband of twenty-three years ten months earlier. She was lonely and fearful that she would always remain so.

Desperate for companionship, Mabel decided to advertise for a partner. She knew other women whose solicitation for a spouse had been answered and a handful of those were fortunate enough to marry the men who replied. Mabel wondered if she would be as lucky. Blinking away tears, she decided the time was right to submit an ad to the popular publication *The New Plan*. Perhaps an equally lonely gentleman would read the personal plea and seek her out. Perhaps she would find love again.

Helping eligible men and women find one another, correspond, and marry was the main goal of *The New Plan*. Published in Kansas City, Missouri, the magazine's purpose was to unite lonely hearts, with various monetary and social backgrounds, who were unable to find a desirable life partner.

Ladies especially, whose opportunities are somewhat limited as to forming acquaintances, seek the method (proposed in The New Plan*) knowing that in no other way have they so much advantage. Don't think because you are not*

wealthy yourself that you cannot get a rich party to marry you. Love is not meas-
ured in lucre. Morality, fidelity, respectability, ambition and beauty often tip
the opposing weight of wealth on the matrimonial scale. Women in affluent cir-
cumstances are not usually seeking an increase of wealth in marriage. The self-
respecting man of means, in seeking a wife is not seeking her for the property she
may have.

We get many inquiries from both sexes who have plenty of means for two
and who seek life companions of true worth and not for means. We do business
with such people constantly and know whereof we speak.

The New Plan Notice—1917

A list of the magazine's aims and methods of business were listed on
the back cover of each edition. The simple and easy-to-follow plan promised
speedy and satisfactory results for all who submitted an advertisement.

Our time and money is devoted entirely to the interest of the unmarried; to
elevate and promote the welfare of marriageable people and furnish a safe,
reliable and confidential method at a nominal cost, whereby good honorable
people, of sincere and moral intentions, may better enable themselves to be-
come acquainted with a large number of such people of the opposite sex as they
may deem worthy of consideration, which may lead to their future happiness
and prosperity.

The New Plan—1917

The personal ads listed in the publication were genuine, and ladies
whose advertisements were published signed a statement in which they
agreed to answer every letter received from interested gentlemen readers
who enclosed postage, either accepting or declining correspondence.

The cost for each advertisement was $1.00. The magazine's editors
boasted that this offer was "the greatest bargain in the world for the
money."

Three unidentfied mail-order brides show off their assets in hopes of attracting marriageable men.

The New Plan was in circulation from 1911 to 1917. The following are samples of advertisements found in the September 1917 edition of the periodical. The first advertisement was submitted by Mabel Haskell.

———— •✦• ————

I am a lonely, unencumbered widow; age 48; weight 165; height, 5 feet 6 inches; big blue eyes; brown hair; fair complexion; American; religion, Methodist. I have property worth $30,000. A sunny disposition; considered very good looking. Would like to hear from some good business man. Object, matrimony.

———— •✦• ————

A very stylish and attractive widow by death, with property worth $3,000. Age 33; weight, 125; height, 5 feet 5 inches; blue eyes; brown hair; complexion, fair; American; good housekeeper and cook. Would marry if I can find a congenial companion. Either city or country life. Will answer all letters containing stamps. Will inherit $6,000.

———— •✦• ————

I am a good looking young lady, a brunette, with velvet brown eyes, brown hair and fair complexion; height, 5 feet 6 inches; weight 141; age, 20. I have a college education and am highly accomplished in music and voice. Have a kind and cheerful disposition and am a lover of home and children. Have means of $20,000 and income of $100 per month.

I desire the acquaintance of good moral men. Any age.

———— •◆• ————

I do not pose as a beauty, but people tell me that I look well. Enjoy fun and social gatherings. Age, 27; weight 138; height, 64 inches; brown eyes; brown hair; fair complexion; American; very good disposition; plain dresser, but neat. Prefer country life. Income $20 per month. Matrimonially inclined.

———— •◆• ————

Everybody says that I'm fine looking for my age; am honest, intelligent, neat and clean, kind-hearted and have a good character. Age, 58; weight, 120; height 5 feet 2 inches; blue eyes; brown hair; fine homemaker. Income, $200 per year. Have real estate worth $4,000. Object matrimony. Will answer all letters.

———— •◆• ————

A winsome miss of 22; very beautiful, jolly and entertaining; fond of home and children; from good family; American; Christian; blue eyes; golden hair; fair complexion; pleasant disposition; play piano. Will inherit $10,000. Also have means of $1,000. None but men of good education need to write from 20 to 38 years of age.

———— •◆• ————

Would like to get married, because I'm lonesome. Am considered rather good looking and of a lovable disposition. Age, 35; height, 5 feet 5 inches; weight 145; hazel eyes; brown hair; American; occupation, stenographer and bookkeeper. Will inherit a few thousand. Will answer all letters.

———— •◆• ————

Society has no charms for me; prefer a quiet life. Am an American lady, with common school education; well thought of and respected; age, 25; height 5 feet 9 inches; weight, 155; blue eyes; light hair. Have means of $3,000. Wish correspondence with good natured, honest, industrious man.

———— •◆• ————

A perfect blonde; trained nurse, wishes to make the acquaintance of a nice young gentlemen, view to matrimony; age 23, weight 124, height 5 feet 3 inches; German-American; college education, very neat dresser; will answer all letters.

———— •◆• ————

Who will be the first to write to this lady of 33 years, weight 100, height 5 feet 2 inches, brown eyes, brown hair, light complexion; occupation dressmaker, fine housekeeper and cook; kind, good-natured disposition; would marry if suited. Country life preferred.

Dear old men, here is your chance to get a true loving companion. I am a widow by death; age 69 years, but don't look or feel or act over 40; always in good humor, very loving and kind; a good housekeeper, weight 104, height 5 feet 2 inches, blue eyes, brown hair, nationality German; would like to meet some congenial gentlemen near my own age, with means enough to make a good home.

Hello, all you widowers and bachelors, right this way if you are looking for a companion; here she is, age 60, weight 100, height 4 feet 11 inches; black eyes, dark hair, American; Golden Rule religion, jolly and good natured; have means of $3,000; wish a husband with some means, city or country, age from 50 to 75; will answer all letters.

Boys, I am a lonesome little girl, alone in the world and earning my own living and am tired of doing so; my age is 20 years, weight 145, height 5 feet 3 inches, blue eyes, dark hair, good housekeeper, am considered good looking, have some means, also piano; common school education; prefer country life; will marry if suited; no Catholics need to write.

Am well known and respected by all; American; Golden Rule religion; age 19, weight 132, height 5 feet 3 inches; dark brown eyes, brown hair, olive complexion; live with my parents; high school education; very musical and trained voice; have means of $6,000; also will inherit; want to become acquainted with moral men, suitable age.

———— •◆• ————

Who wants to correspond with a jolly little blonde, a lover of peace and harmony; always tries to make others happy; age 22, weight 115, height 5 feet 2 inches, light hair, blue eyes, fair complexion; wish to hear from true, honest gentlemen of good character. All worthy letters answered.

———— •◆• ————

Would like to hear from a man of good business ability and of neat, personal appearance. I am 33 years of age, weight 117, height 5 feet 4 inches, blue eyes and brown hair, American, common school education, good personal appearance, fond of home and children, do not care for society, have property worth $1,000.

———— •◆• ————

Here is a pretty blonde with pretty blue eyes; very fair complexion; good education; modest by occupation; age 28; weight, 160; height 5 feet 9 inches; very neat and fond of home. Wish to hear from business man or farmer with his own farm. Lover of home and children. Will answer all letters. Will inherit.

———— •◆• ————

Gentlemen, I am in earnest; would like to hear from men of good character and reputation who need and would appreciate a good trustworthy woman; am 45 years old, weight 130, height 5 feet 5 inches, blue eyes, black hair; nationality Mexican; have property worth $500; will inherit $2,000. Will correspond for matrimony.

———— •◆• ————

Here comes a sweet lady from the land of flowers and sunshine; age 35; weight 150, height 5 feet 8 inches; brown eyes, brown hair, rosy complexion; a musician, occupation, real estate. Have income also some means. Object matrimony.

———— •◆• ————

I am in every way qualified to appreciate and care for a good partner and home. Am healthy, of neat appearance, affectionate and genial disposition. Age 20, weight 123, height 5 feet 5 inches, dark brown eyes and hair. Thoroughly competent in housework and farming. Will inherit. Answer all letters.

———— •◆• ————

American girl; farmer's daughter; raised on the farm, own 40 acres of land; father owns 100. Would consider marriage if I can find some good honest man, no objections to widower with one or two children. My age is 22; weight, 160; height 5 feet 6 inches; black hair and eyes. Write and learn more.

———— •◆• ————

Am a home loving lady never was married, am lonely and wish to hear from a good man who loves home life. I am German American; age 30; weight, 140; height 5 feet 4 inches; blue eyes; light hair; fair complexion. Have some real estate. Prefer city life. Matrimonially inclined.

———— •◆• ————

A widow of refinement and education would be pleased to hear from gentlemen, one who is not looking for money, but for a companion. Am a well read woman, traveled ten years for a firm and have been all over U.S.A. Age 50, weight 160, height 5 feet 2 inches; dark blue eyes, dark hair mixed with gray. Nationality English-Scotch. Will answer all letters containing stamps.

———— •◆• ————

Boys, you'll enjoy receiving my letters, for I'm a jolly girl. Age, 24; weight, 130; height 5 feet 5 inches; brown eyes; blonde hair, nationality, French; Catholic religion; occupation, stenographer; income, $1,000; play violin. Will write for fun or matrimony. Catholic preferred.

———— ·◆· ————

If any of the advertisements resulted in matrimony, the subscriber and author of the ad agreed to pay a $5.00 service fee to the magazine.

We aid our members in every way possible to find their "ideal" and expect they will be prompt in paying us when they find the person of their choice, as we receive nothing for our time and labor until marriage occurs. We realize that we have something to do and will work faithfully.

The New Plan—1917

AFTERWORD

*T*hroughout the mid-1800s, adventurous men from Boston to Georgia rushed west to lay claim to parts of the wild frontier. They came to farm, trap, ranch, and establish businesses. Those who heard the California streams were lined with gold came to find their fortune. While some found riches, many struggled winter after winter, unable to find a single nugget. Prosperous or poor, all at one time or another were lonesome, longing for the stability only the company of a woman could provide.

As there were very few available women living in the West, the only option was to attract women from the East. In an effort to entice the female population to the unsettled land, unique methods were employed. Men sought prospective brides through churches back home, letters to available schoolteachers, and advertisements in newspapers and magazines.

The practice of seeking a bride in this manner continued on into the turn of the century. Women in the East and the Midwest responded to ads, exchanged letters and photos, and eventually agreed to marry men they had never met. Ranchers like John Bartly of North Dakota had doubts that he would find a wife through an advertisement. After his friends assured him there was a chance it could happen, he reluctantly placed an ad in a Pennsylvania newspaper.

The article on page four of the May 8, 1912, edition of a North Dakota newspaper proved that Bartly's friends were right and restored his faith in want ads.

Reverend C.L. Wallace of the Methodist church solemnized a marriage last evening which is the happy culmination of a novel but ardent courtship. About a year and a half ago, John Bartly, a prosperous farmer of Newbre Township and the step son of P.W. Hinebaugh, advertised in some rural paper for a wife with which to share his prosperity and comfortable home. He stated the fact that he was the owner of a well stocked farm of 640 acres of Ramsey County land. The advertisement found its way to McIntosh, Minnesota, where Mrs. C. E. Davis, who is devoted to her grand daughter, Margery, and is desirous that the young girl should enjoy some of the luxuries of life which she could not afford to give her, answered the advertisement without consulting the young lady.

When the gentlemen's answer came, it not only pleased the fond parent, but met the approval of Miss Davis and immediately a lively correspondence with an exchange of photographs sprung up. This continued a year and by that time the young man decided that Miss Davis was the girl he wanted and asked her to come to North Dakota and be his wife. He wrote the grandmother at the same time assuring her of the sincerity and desires to give her grandchild a good home.

The date was set and the young lady, accompanied by Mrs. Davis, reached Lakota last evening. It was agreed before hand that each should wear a bouquet of flowers so that there would be no difficulty in recognizing one another. Mr. Bartly was at the depot at Lakota with a large number of friends. It was a case of complete satisfaction and they lost no time in coming to the county seat to secure the license, and have the ceremony performed. It occurred at the Sevilla Hotel last evening and the bride looked very attractive in a suit of dark blue serge with a veil of bridal net caught with a wreath and carrying a large bridal bouquet.

Mr. and Mrs. Mallough who are residents of the Sevilla, consented to be the attendants and it was a very impressive scene. Had it not been the busy season of the year the groom would have had a more elaborate wedding with a reception at his large country home, but under the circumstances it was a very quiet affair.

The Devils Lake Daily Journal—1912

Not everyone who favorably answered mail-order bride advertisements enjoyed happily-ever-after endings. In the case of a bachelor from Buford,

North Dakota, the wedding was called off shortly after the engaged couple met.

Strange indeed was the experience of two girls aged nineteen and twenty years, who reached this city on Saturday without money and absolutely helpless.

As the story goes, the two girls left their homes, for they are not sisters, several weeks ago to come to Buford, North Dakota. One of the girls has been corresponding with a farmer living near Buford and their correspondence had progressed to the point where he had popped the question.

The girl immediately started for Buford from far away New York, but her friend insisted on accompanying her, probably with the hope that she, too, would become entangled matrimonially. But when they arrived at Buford and the elder of the two had gazed upon the face of the man with whom she had been corresponding the spell was immediately broken. He didn't suit. In fact he wouldn't do at all. The other girl fully acquiesced in the decision and so they started back again.

As girls will do, they carried all their money in one pocketbook and in some way this was lost with the result that they reached Grand Forks financially embarrassed to say the least. They took the only course they could take under the circumstances and told their story to Chief Lowe. Through his aid and that of other interested citizens enough money was raised to send them at least a long way on their return trip to Rochester.

They are sadder and wiser girls than when they left home and it is hardly likely that they will ever again, no matter what matrimonial stringency may come, try the correspondence route to matrimony.

The Wahpeton Times, North Dakota—March 9, 1911

In spite of the occasional mismatch or short-lived union, historians at the National Archive Department in Washington believe that mail-order brides produced a high percentage of permanent marriages. The reason cited is that the advertisements were candid and direct in their explanations of exactly what was wanted and expected from a prospective spouse. And if requested, the parties involved sent accurate photos of themselves along with a page of background information. Often, when the pair met, the groom-to-be signed an agreement, witnessed by three upstanding members of the territory, not to abuse or mistreat the bride-to-be. The prospective bride then signed a paper (also witnessed) not to nag or try to change the intended.

Desperate bachelors and pining maidens were willing to consent to whatever terms were necessary in order to secure a spouse. The scarcity of females in the West and the rapidly changing times forced traditional thinking women and men to succumb to new ways of finding a mate. Mail-order couples wed in hopes that their mutually beneficial marriage would develop into love. History records that many times the result was, indeed, a happily-ever-after life for both.

BIBLIOGRAPHY

Mary Richardson Walker

Butruille, Susan G. *Women's Voices from the Western Frontier.* Boise, Idaho: Tamarack Books, Inc., 1995.

Drury, Clifford M. *Elkanah and Mary Walker: Pioneers Among the Spokanes.* Caldwell, Idaho: The Caxton Printers, 1940.

Elkanah and Mary Richardson Walker Papers, 1830-1938. Washington State University Library. Selected material from the Walker Library Collection.

Luchetti, Cathy & Olwell, Carol. *Women of the West.* Berkeley, California: Antelope Island Press, 1982.

Eleanor Berry

Boessenecker, John. "The Bride and the Brigand." *The California Historical Magazine.* San Francisco, California: California Historical Society, March/April 1987.

Johnson, Dorothy. *Some Went West.* New York: Dodd, Mead & Company, 1965.

Ketcham, Barbara. *A Bride Who Went West.* New York: Avon Books, 1980.

Morley, Jim & Foley, Doris. *Gold Cities.* Berkeley, California: Howell-North Books, 1965.

Starkey, Marilyn & Browne, Juanita K. *Sketches of Yesterday and Today in Nevada County.* Nevada City, California: Nevada County Historical Society, 1988.

Asa Mercer

Bagley, Clarence B. *History of Seattle.* Chicago, Illinois: S.J. Publishing Co., 1916.

Bagley, Clarence B. "The Mercer Immigration: Two Cargoes of Maidens for the Sound Country." *The Quarterly of the Oregon Historical Society.* March 1904.

Blankenship, George. *Lights and Shades of Pioneer Life on Puget Sound.* Olympia, Washington: 1923.

Conant, Roger. "Mercer's Belles." *The Journal of a Reporter Pullman.* Seattle, Washington: Washington State University Press, 1962.

Corning, Howard McKinley. *The New Washington: A Guide to the Evergreen State.* Washington State Historical Society, Portland, Oregon: Metropolitan Press, 1950.

Engle, Flora A.P. "The Story of the Mercer Expeditions." *Washington Historical Quarterly.* Seattle, Washington: October 1915.

Hines, Reverend H.K. *An Illustrated History of the State of Washington.* Chicago, Illinois: Lewis Publishing Co., 1893.

Prosch, Charles. *Reminiscences of Washington Territory.* Fairfield, Washington: Ye Galleon Press, 1995.

Sayre, J. Willis. *This City of Ours.* Seattle, Washington: Board of Directors Seattle School District No. 1, 1936.

Seattle Post Intelligencer. Seattle, Washington. June 25, 1899; December 30, 1900; February 2, 1901.

Told by the Pioneers: Frontier Life as Told by Those Who Remember the Days of the Territory and Early Statehood of Washington. The State Association of the Daughters of the Pioneers of Washington, N.D., 1937.

Volume of Memoirs and Genealogy of Representative Citizens of the City of Seattle and County of King, Washington. New York: Lewis Publishing Company, 1903.

Watt, Roberta Frye. *Four Wagons West: The Story of Seattle.* Seattle, Washington: Binford & Mort, 1931.

Phoebe Harrington

Arrington, Leonard J. *History of Idaho.* Boise, Idaho: University of Idaho Press, 1994.

Pomeroy, Earl S. *The Pacific Slope.* Reno, Nevada: University of Nevada Press, 2003.

Studebaker, William V. *Short of a Good Promise.* Pullman, Washington: Washington State University Press, 1999.

Bethenia Owens-Adair

Korn, Jerry. *The Women.* Alexandria, Virginia: Time Incorporated, 1979.

Lockley, Fred. *With Her Own Wings.* Portland, Oregon: Beattie and Company Printers, 1948.

Luchetti, Cathy. *I Do.* New York: Random House, 1996.

Luchetti, Cathy & Olwell, Carol. *Women of the West.* Berkeley, California: Antelope Island Press, 1982.

Owens-Adair, Bethenia. *Gleanings from a Pioneer Woman Physician's Life.* Portland, Oregon: Mann & Beach, 1906.

Owens-Adair, Bethenia. *Papers of a Physician, 1864–1921.* Collection on file at the Oregon State University.

The Benton Brides

Brown, Dee. *Wondrous Times on the Frontier.* New York: HarperCollins Publishers, 1992.

Cross, Mary Bywater. *Quilts of the Oregon Trail.* Nashville, Tennessee: Rutledge Hill Press, 2000.

Dodds, Linda & Buan, Carolyn. *Portland Then and Now.* San Francisco: Thunder Bay Press, 2001.

Republican Standard Newspaper. Ellicott City, Maryland. February 1865–November 1865 editions.

Rachel Bella Kahn

Daley, Janet. *North Dakota History, Journal of the Northern Plains.* Fargo, North Dakota: State Historical Society of North Dakota, 2000.

Kalinowski, Andrea. *Stories Untold: Jewish Pioneer Women.* Sante Fe, New Mexico: Museum of New Mexico Press, 2002.

Luchetti, Cathy. *I Do.* New York: Random House, Inc., 1996.

Rikoon, J. Sanford. *Rachel Calof's Story.* Bloomington, Indiana: Indiana University Press, 1995.

Robinson, Elwyn B. *History of North Dakota.* Fargo, North Dakota: North Dakota State University, 1995.

Elinore Pruitt Stewart

Butruille, Susan G. *Women's Voices from the Western Frontier.* Boise, Idaho: Tamarack Books, Inc., 1995.

Korn, Jerry. *The Women.* Alexandria, Virginia: Time Incorporated, 1979.

Stewart, Elinore P. *Letters of a Woman Homesteader.* Boston: Houghton Mifflin Company, 1913.

Stewart, Elinore P. *Letters on an Elk Hunt.* Boston: Houghton Mifflin Company, 1912.

Eliza Farnham

Bancroft, H.H. *History of California.* Santa Cruz, California: Mountain Network News, 1886 Vol. XX, p. 734

Barriga, Joan. "Survival with Style: The Women of the Santa Cruz Mountains." *Mountain Network News,* August, 2002.

Farnham, Eliza W. *California, In-doors and Out.* New York: Hes & De Graf Publishing, 1856.

Herr, Pamela. *Reformer: The Women Who Made the West.* New York: Avon Books, 1980.

Korn, Jerry, ed. *The Women On the New Career Trail.* Alexandria, Virginia: Time Incorporated, 1979.

Lewis, David W. *Eliza Woodson Burhans Farnham: Notable American Women.* Cambridge, Massachusetts: Harvard University Press, 1971.

"Women Arrive." *Alta California Newspaper.* November 3, 1851.

Kathleen Forreststall

Carter, William. *Ghost Towns of the West*. Menlo Park, California: Lane Publishing, 1971.

Convis, Charles. *True Tales of the Old West*. Carson City, Nevada: Pioneer Press, 1998.

"Irish Brides." *San Francisco Historical Society Quarterly*, Vol. 18, 1982.

Lawliss, Chuck. *Ghost Towns, Gamblers and Gold*. New York: Gallery Books, 1985.

Steber, Rick. *Women of the West*. Prineville, Oregon: Bonanza Publishing, 1988.

They Came From County Cork, 5th ed. Oregon Historical Research Library: Walla Walla, Oregon, 1965.

Additional Reference Material

"A Happy Ride." *Nevada County Historical Bulletin*, Vol. 7 No. 3, 1975.

"A History of Jerome and Surrounding Areas." *Idaho State Historical News*, Edition 12, 1951.

Lardner, William & Brock, M.J. *History of Placer and Nevada Counties*. Los Angeles: Historic Record Company, 1924.

"Marriage Customs in Early California." *The Californians Magazine*, November/December 1991.

ABOUT THE AUTHOR

Chris Enss is an award-winning screen writer who has written for television, short subject films, live performances, and for the movies. She is the co-author (with JoAnn Chartier) of The Globe Pequot Press's *Love Untamed: True Romances Stories of the Old West, Gilded Girls: Women Entertainers of the Old West,* and *She Wore A Yellow Ribbon: Women Patriots and Soldiers of the Old West* and *The Cowboy and the Senorita* and *Happy Trails* (with Howard Kazanjian). Her research and writing reveals the funny, touching, exciting, and tragic stories of historical and contemporary times.

Enss has done everything from stand-up comedy to working as a stunt person at the Old Tucson Movie Studio. She learned the basics of writing for film and television at the University of Arizona, and she is currently working with *Return of the Jedi* producer Howard Kazanjian on the movie version of *The Cowboy and the Senorita,* their biography of western stars Roy Rogers and Dale Evans.

 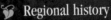